# A PURPLE

# *Rose*

# ROMANCE

PHYLLIS FRANK

Fulton Books, Inc.
Meadville, PA

Published by Fulton Books 2020

ISBN 978-1-64654-914-6 (paperback)
ISBN 978-1-64654-915-3 (digital)

Printed in the United States of America

For my husband, Gary. I love him with all my heart and couldn't have made it a day in this life without him.

And for my dear friend, Carol, who's sincere words during a casual conversation erased all my doubts about continuing with this book.

# CHAPTER 1

## The Beginning: Purple Rose

Her eyes opened. She had fallen asleep on the couch. The 5:00 a.m. light was out there. The panic sets in as it did every morning, deep within her. When will the depression catch hold of her, and she won't be able to get away? She woke up consumed in anxiety, sadness, and disappointment that she is awake. The desperate feeling of depression had been deeper and stronger every single day that she awakened. It could end in a matter of minutes if she chose. She was afraid she would, and afraid she wouldn't. It was the loneliness and isolation she felt every day, and it killed her inside. Hers was not a glorious issue.

She was everyone's worst nightmare. If only the doctors would have listened to her, she may have at least had a chance at remaining normal. Nobody seemed to care. After it was all over, one of her doctors said how she didn't see that she was so sick. Did this doctor really think all this was just to get attention?

"Get up and get moving, so it can't catch you. If it does, you may not be able to get away from it," she told herself.

She looked at her dogs, who were standing by the couch, wagging their tails. She smiled and told them, "Okay, Ricky and Honey, we'll go out and get breakfast in a few." She looked over at her two cats, who were sleeping on the edge of the couch. She shook her head and looked at Ricky and Honey. "Chubbs and Huxley sure know

5

how to take life easy." She knew her animals needed her, but she couldn't deal with the devastating depression. It got harder every day.

Ricky was a brown-and-white English Springer Spaniel, and Honey was a very old, small, tan-and-white mixed breed. Her left ear would stand up, the right one wouldn't. Honey walked with a permanent limp, and she had multiple health issues. Leah's cats were typical domestic short-hair cats, black and white, cute as can be. Chubbs was cross-eyed. Huxley was smaller and silly. Chubbs was the oldest of the litter and Huxley the youngest. Funny, they acted it. They didn't wake up until absolutely necessary. She had to smile. Her animals were her reasons to get out of bed and do something for someone who needed her. Without them, there would be no thought given to what she wanted to happen. "Okay, let's go out." Ricky leaped to his feet and ran to the door. Honey had trouble standing and needed to be carried. Leah picked her up gently and kissed her.

Chubbs and Huxley finally opened their eyes, but didn't move. They knew Leah would put their breakfast out for them, and they would eat when they felt like it.

She had to get going and face the day. The worst part of it was that when she seemed to beat this. She felt good for a period of time. She thought the overwhelming control it had on her was over. She could do this. If she pretended hard enough, she could almost convince herself that the past twenty-two years hadn't really happened, and that she was normal. Then, the depression slowly creeped back. It seemed to get her from behind and then beat her to the ground. All she wanted to do was die. She wanted to end it, but she was afraid that if she failed, it would only be worse. She was totally drained. She had no energy left to deal. The depth of it all was so painful and totally exhausting. She couldn't face herself. The sadness she felt was more than she ever thought possible. She felt totally alone. She felt ugly and repulsive, because she was. She had a look in her eyes that only her best friend would notice and understand. It was a look of being constantly on edge and feeling nonhuman. She could hide it from others very well. She's had a lot of practice.

She loves old romantic and noir films from the 1940s '50s, '60s and '70s and television crime shows from the 1970s, '80s, and early

'90s. She would watch and disappear in a world of make-believe. She could forget for a while who, or better yet, forget *what* she was. Then, the one part that always jolted her back to reality was when that beautiful girl got that guy, they'd fallen in love during the story line. He held that beautiful girl and he kissed her. That girl dropped her clothes in front of him. He reached out and held her close. They always seemed to end up in bed. It made her cry every time. She'd never feel beautiful again. No man would want to hold her or kiss her like that, let alone bring her to bed with him. She would never have that moment in her life with any man. She hoped every night that she wouldn't wake up the next day, but she always did. She cried every morning. Getting through the day was hard, most times, too hard. She couldn't stand being who and what she was. She wished she were dead.

Early in the evening, a car pulled up to the house and blew the horn. She looked out the window and then opened the door, came out, ran to the car, and got in. "Hi, Julie. Sorry I'm so late," she said. "Again, more damn problems." Leah was thin, had beautiful auburn hair, shoulder length, green/brown eyes, and a very petite frame. Her face was pretty. She had a natural beauty.

"Leah, don't worry about it. The party just started a while ago. I love your perfume," Julie answered and smiled.

"Thanks. It's Oscar de la Renta. At least I smell good. I can't do without my perfume. Do I look all right?" Leah said, and pulled a bottle of water out of her purse. She popped something in her mouth and took a drink of her water.

"I saw that," Julie said. Julie was average size. Very pretty. She had light brown hair, a little longer than Leah's, beautiful dark eyes. A beautiful girl without a doubt. One of the natural beauties.

"Yeah, well, whatever. I can't calm down. I swear I wish I were dead," Leah said, and took another swallow of water.

Julie tapped Leah's hand. "Let's just get to my place and have a good time. You'll enjoy yourself. It's a beautiful evening to have a garden party for no good reason other than being with our friends. All our old riding buddies are there, and some of Rob's friends that you know."

"Okay," Leah said. "You're right, it'll be a nice night. I'm sorry."

Julie laughed. "I understand, and don't worry. Let's just have a great time, okay?'

Leah nodded in agreement. Leah thought to herself, *No one understands.*

They pulled up to Julie's house. It was a nice ranch home. Julie and Leah got out of the car and walked around to the fenced in backyard. The air was sweet. Music was playing. Leah looked around and saw many of their old friends. As they walked into the yard, Julie said, "Come on, let's get something to drink."

"Great," Leah said. They walked over to the bar, and Julie poured two glasses of white wine. She handed one to Leah. Leah took a big gulp. Julie looked around, and was a little puzzled.

Leah noticed the look on her face and asked, "What's wrong?"

Julie had made seating arrangements, and this was not what she had planned. She knew Leah would panic if she wasn't seated with people she was comfortable with. At any rate, she said, "Nothing. Let's find someplace for you to sit. I thought I had set you up some-where else, but it looks like things have changed for some reason. Maybe Rob misunderstood the arrangement."

As they walked through the crowd, people were glad to see Leah. It was good to see them also. Leah had many great memories of her riding days. "Oh, Leah," Julie said, "there's an empty place over at that table in the back corner. C'mon, I'll walk you over."

Leah looked, and there were five people sitting there and, of course, the empty seat. She began to feel anxious and panicked. *I hate when this happens to me,* she thought to herself. She took a big sip of her wine as they approached the table. The table was draped in an off-white satin tablecloth. Flower petals were scattered on it, along with confetti of stars and hearts. The centerpiece was a small dish with a candle.

"Leah, you know Marie, Tom, Ann, and Dave, Rob's friends," Julie said.

The song "Strange Magic" by ELO began to play. Leah noticed the song since it was one of her favorites. The words helped her smile and look calm as she noticed there was also a man at the table that she hadn't met or seen before. He was a bit older than she and Julie. He was a very heavy man, balding, had dark hair, and a dark mustache. His eyes were blue, a beautiful shade of blue. He had a gentle roughness about him. She didn't do well with new people. Julie looked at the man and said, "Leah Turner, this is Bill Stone. Bill Stone, this is Leah Turner."

Bill smiled. He had a nice smile also. He stood and pulled the empty chair that was next to him out for Leah to sit down. Bill stood about five eight. "Nice to meet you, Leah," he said. He had a soft, deep, gentle voice that fit him perfectly.

Their eyes met. He smiled at Leah. She felt as if time stood still. A calm, quiet feeling wrapped around her. Leah smiled and barely got the words out but said, "Nice to meet you too." She sat down. "Thank you," she said while thinking to herself, *Where did this man come from? No one pulls a chair out for a girl anymore.*

"My pleasure," Bill said and sat back down.

Leah looked at him again, and she could see a sadness deep within him, although he still smiled and graciously conversed with the others at the table.

It was beginning to get dark. Music played, and Leah said, "Julie and Rob have a great collection of music." She took a big sip of wine to calm her nerves.

Bill smiled. "Yes, they do. That song 'Strange Magic' has interesting lyrics."

"Yes, it does," she said. They smiled at each other.

Leah noticed that the stars were beginning to come out. The grill was full of all sorts of things. Rob was grilling like a professional chef. He was over six feet tall, had a perfect build, great face, nice reddish-brown hair—a stunning-looking man. He was one of those who didn't really know it, though. There was a table to the side of the grill filled with even more delicious food, flowers, and candles. Lights were strung through the trees.

Ann said to Leah, "So how have you been? It's great seeing you again."

Leah smiled. "Good to see you too, Ann. It's been way too long." She never said how she'd been. Leah figured that Ann really didn't want to hear it all. After taking another sip of her wine, she turned to Bill. "So how do you know Julie and Rob?" She usually wasn't so quick to talk to someone she didn't know. *It must be the wine and candy I had already to make me act this way. I wish I could do this on my own,* she thought to herself.

He just smiled and said, "Oh, we met years ago. We became good friends over time. I had gone to California for a while and lost touch."

Just then, Julie walked over. She overheard part of the conversation and said, "We met way before you and I met, and good friends is an understatement, Leah. This man has been such a godsend to me and Rob. We don't know what we would have done without him back then." She put her arms around Bill's shoulders and kissed him on the cheek.

"You make more of it than it is, Julie, but thank you," Bill said and sipped his drink. He chuckled softly.

"Thanks for coming tonight, Bill," Julie said. She looked at everyone at the table and said, "Dinner is ready, so please go help yourselves."

Everyone at the table got up to get dinner. Leah and Bill were last to get up. Bill got up and put his hand on Leah's chair, so she could get up. She noticed how neatly and how perfectly dressed he was. A blue shirt, top button open, a gray suit jacket and gray pants. She looked at him and smiled. *He really is very handsome,* she thought to herself. She doubted her outfit, a black shirt and tan slacks and black flip-flops. She never really dressed up. She never felt pretty. She thought to herself, *I hope I look all right.*

"So how do you know Julie?" Bill asked. They walked to the table, and he stepped aside and motioned for Leah get her dinner first.

*He's so polite,* Leah thought. "Riding horses," she said and began filling her plate.

"Oh? Riding horses?" Bill said and took a plate for himself.

"Yes. We became friends very quickly. She's my best friend." Leah smiled. "When my horse, Socrates, died, I stopped going to the barn, but we kept in touch. It hurt too much to be at the barn.

All those memories were too hard to face. Julie would call to check on me and try to get me to go back." She continued to fill her plate. "It was early October, and finally I did go back to exercise a friend's horse. That made Julie happy, and I think she arranged the whole thing, to be honest. She's a good friend." Leah took another spoonful of food and continued, "Then, one day, I see this horse in a stall, and realized I'd seen him every time I was there, just standing in that stall. He was always hanging his head in the corner."

Bill began to fill his plate and looked at hers and laughed. "I'm sorry, where do you put it?"

Leah looked at Bill and asked, "Where do I put what?"

"All that food. It's just you're so…so tiny, and that's a huge plate you have there. I don't mean to laugh. I have a hefty appetite too, but it's obvious with me."

Leah looked at her plate. She had to laugh. "I guess I did take a lot, didn't I? I'm hungry. I take after my great grandmother. She was tiny, and one hundred pounds soaking wet. I never knew her. Just saw pictures of her way back in the day." She paused and asked, "Am I talking too much?"

"Oh no, not at all." Bill smiled.

Leah smiled slightly and said, "Really?"

Bill laughed and said, "Really."

They walked back to the table. Leah was relieved and still surprised she could be this comfortable around a perfect stranger. "So anyway, that's when I met my next horse and came back to the barn." Just as she sat down, Leah realized she hadn't gotten more wine. "I'll be right back," she said, "I need some more wine." And she meant it. She didn't want this "calm" to go away. The wine and candy were helping her to keep the anxiety and depression that was looming inside of her manageable for the time being.

Bill hadn't sat down yet. He put his plate down. "I'll get it for you. Be right back," Bill said and walked away.

Leah smiled and said, "Oh, that's so nice, thanks."

Marie smiled at Leah. "So what do you think of Bill?"

"He's very nice. Julie's face said it all about how she feels about him. And I think he's very handsome." Leah said.

Marie seemed surprised for a second at Leah's response. "He is very nice," she said.

Bill came back with a glass of wine for Leah. "Here you go," he said and set it down by her plate and sat down.

"Thank you," she said. She took a huge sip and began to eat. She tried to adjust her seat and, in doing so, hit the table and Bill's drink spilled, just slightly. She grabbed a napkin. "Great, I'm sorry. I'm so clumsy. Worse than a bull in a china shop, I swear." She began to dab the tablecloth with her napkin.

Bill shook his head, laughed, and said, "Don't worry about it," and he gently took the napkin from her and tried to clean the table-cloth. "You're fine. It'll just leave a little stain." He looked at her, smiled and said, "We left our mark." Their eyes met again, for a long time. Leah just smiled slightly. For a second, she couldn't breathe.

Leah looked at the stain. It was in the shape of a heart. "Look, it looks like a heart!" She put her hand on her forehead and said, "I'm sorry. I don't seem to have any filter tonight. I feel so silly."

Bill laughed. "Don't feel silly, and yes, it does." He enjoyed that she was so spontaneous.

"What are you drinking anyway?" Leah asked. Then she thought to herself, *Leah, shut up already.* It was obvious to herself that she couldn't.

Whiskey," he replied. "Would you like a taste?" Bill offered her his glass.

Much to her surprise, because she would never drink from a glass that someone she didn't know had, but in spite of herself, Leah said, "Sure." She couldn't seem to stop herself tonight. *What the hell is going on with me?* she thought.

He handed the glass to her. She took the glass, took a drink, and began to choke and gasp for air. Leah could barely get the words out, but managed to say, "This is poison!"

Everyone at the table laughed.

"You could have said no," Bill said, laughing so hard he could barely talk. He realized she didn't drink like that, obviously. "I'm sorry, really."

Leah had to laugh. "I should have said no. That stuff is awful! I didn't know anything could taste that terrible!"

"Are you all right?" Bill said, feeling bad about laughing at her.

There was something very charming about Bill that Leah couldn't pinpoint. She wondered how Julie and Rob met him. "Yes, I'm okay. Just choking to death. That's all."

He smiled and said, "You can't just gulp that stuff down if you aren't used to it. I'm sorry, I didn't realize..."

Leah smiled. "It's okay. Just make sure you come to my funeral when this stuff really hits."

"You're a good sport," Bill said. "I'm sorry."

Eventually, everyone at the table finished their dinner and began to mingle. Leah still had food on her plate that she was working on. She was a slow eater.

"So finish telling me about the horses." Bill said. "You used to ride?"

"Yes, I used to. I really loved it, but I wasn't very good at it."

"Somehow I think you were," Bill said.

Leah shrugged her shoulders. "Maybe," she said and took another forkful of her dinner. Then she looked at Bill's plate. "What's that?" she said as she motioned to some kind of salad. "I missed that one."

"Some kind of vegetable something. It's good. Here, have some," Bill said.

Again, this was something she would never do with someone she didn't know. But regardless, she said, "Thanks," and reached over and took a big forkful. "Yum! Whatever it is, it's very good!" She drank more of her wine.

"Glad you like it," Bill said, shaking his head and laughing. "You sure can pack it away. Please, tell me more about your horses."

Leah giggled. "Really? I keep getting off track."

Bill smiled at her. "Yes, I want to hear all about them."

Leah shook her head and smiled. "Anyway, that horse in the stall was pathetic looking. The stall plate had his name on it. King. He didn't look like a king to me. He was so sad. I don't know what happened, but the next thing I knew I was standing in his stall, face-to-face with the biggest set of sad eyes I had ever seen. To this day I don't remember opening the door and going in. I asked him if he'd like to be my next horse," Leah stopped. "Oh boy, you probably think I'm looney or something."

Bill smiled at her. "No, not at all. Maybe it was your horse, Socrates, who guided you." Bill got very serious and said. "One never knows about that kind of thing…connection of souls, I mean." He paused for a second. "What did he say?"

Leah loved that he seemed to understand. She couldn't believe this man. She smiled and said, "Well, he said yes," and Leah giggled again. "Not with his voice, but with his eyes. Then I went to see the barn manager to find out what the story was with him. She told me he was from Upstate New York, very hard to deal with because he didn't get along with other horses, so he had to be turned out alone, which is pathetic in itself because horses are pack animals, they need friends. Companions. You know, loneliness is awful when you understand it, let alone when you don't know why you are put alone. He was also chronically lame, so he was going to be put to sleep the first of November. So I told her I wanted him. She made me wait out the month and ride him and work with him. Well, riding him was like riding a three-legged horse. I wasn't on him five minutes, and he tripped and we both almost kissed the dust. I got off and she looked at me and said that's what she wanted me to see. I told her I wanted him anyway. She wouldn't budge, but finally November rolled around and she sold him to me for a dollar. She was looking out for his best interests. She didn't want him to be put in a situation that wouldn't be his fault. I understood that, but I also knew he was the horse for me. Anyway, that was the best deal I ever made. We were together for fifteen years. So after he was legally mine, a very good friend of mine suggested we see how King and his horse would get along because he didn't believe the rumors of King not being able to be with other horses. King was so gentle and hung on my every word and action. So we turned them out together and everything was fine. He just needed stability and lots of love. Kind of the same with people, isn't it?" Leah paused for a second, and continued, "Anyway, my friend's horse's name was Key. He became King's best friend. Key was a very gentle bay horse, a thoroughbred. An ex racehorse. Then, one day, years later, Key just died. Just like that. King was distraught. They get very attached to each other, very bonded. They call for each other when separated, which was what King did for days. It was gut-wrenching. Eventually, Key's owner moved to another barn and bought another horse. I knew King needed another friend, so I looked at horse rescues and found a gorgeous horse. Next thing I know, Cash, that was his name, came home. Cash was a beautiful gray, in other words, white. He died eleven months after King, and that's how Harry, my horse now, came into my life. Anyway, the day before King died, I of course was at the barn that night taking care of both horses." She paused. "I'm talking too much, aren't I?"

Bill smiled at her. "No, you aren't. I know nothing about horses, but have always thought they are beautiful animals and have been very curious about them. Please, don't stop. I'm really enjoying your story."

Leah looked at Bill. He is such a gentle person, yet so tough in some sort of way. "Okay, if you really do want to hear it all..."

Bill smiled at her and nodded his head. "I really do."

"Well, I always took care of King first because he was mine first. Then, I'd go to Cash and take care of him. King would mosey over and nudge Cash out of the way when he felt time was up. Too funny."

Bill laughed.

"So this particular night, I'm in the field and I'm brushing Cash and talking to him, and I actually heard, in an almost ghostly voice, "You go ahead and love that horse." I looked over, and King made no attempt to nudge him away. He was looking at me, and I knew he was ready to leave this life. Animals get a certain look in their eyes when they're ready to die. I kissed Cash and went over to King. I told him I understood and that I would call the vet tomorrow. I told him I'd spend time with him first. I hugged him, kissed him, told him I love him, and walked away. I knew it was the last time I'd say good night to him and get to see him the next day." Leah's eyes filled with tears. She didn't cry, though.

Bill looked at her. She knew he understood her and wasn't thinking she was crazy. She thought his eyes watered a little.

"So I went to work the next morning, told my boss I had to call the vet and leave a little early so I could put King so sleep. I wasn't at work for ten minutes and my phone rang. It was the barn. They told me King was down and not able to get up. Obviously, I called the vet right then and there and went to the barn and waited with King while he just lay there in the field for what was our last few hours together. I sat down with him, and I kept hugging him and talking quietly to him."

"Oh boy. That must have been rough on you," Bill said.

"Yes, but at least it was a peaceful death. He told me he was ready, and we had the best time together for all those years. It was a beautiful day in August, and we just spent time together until the vet came." Leah looked down for a second.

"How old was he when he died?" Bill asked. He could tell by the look on her face how much she loved and still missed this horse.

"Just shy of thirty-three years. God, I loved him so much," she said.

"I can tell. He was one lucky horse," Bill said and smiled at her.

Leah shook her head, "No, I was the lucky one. It was a very bad time in my life when we first met, and, well, let's just say he saved my life. We needed each other. Socrates held me together during that awful time. He was my escape, my peace. When he died, oh boy. I didn't know what to do. I cried forever, or at least that's how it seemed. I was so depressed, and that's why Julie was so pushy to get me to come to the barn. So when King came along, well, like I said, we needed each other."

Bill noticed she was tearing up. "We don't have to talk about this if—"

Leah quickly said, "No, it's fine. He was so special. I felt like I was nothing, and he was being discarded because he was, I guess, to everyone, nothing. No one wanted him. He was everything to me. Everything." Leah took a deep breath and continued, "That's a terrible feeling, not to be wanted I mean. It just makes me so sad that living things are discarded because they're old, or not perfect. It scares me. Really scares me. It's not just animals either."

"I agree, it's scary." Bill said and Leah knew he understood. That made her like him even more.

"What'd he looked like?" Bill asked.

"Oh, he was beautiful. He was huge. He stood 16.1 hands,"

Bill interrupted, "I'm sorry, but what is 16.1?"

Leah giggled. "Oh, I'm sorry." She stood up and put her hand about a foot above her head. "That's about 16.1 hands."

"Oh, okay. Interesting." Bill said.

Leah continued, "He had a blond forelock. Sort of like bangs on a person, and was what you call a sorrel horse. It took me some time to gain his trust. He had, if I remember correctly, four owners in a year." Leah smiled and said as she finished the last bit of food on her plate, "His full name was The King of Hearts. We all just called him King."

"That's a great name. I can see he won yours." Bill said.

"Yes, he did. I just wish all living things were treated with respect and kindness," Leah said and had a distant smile on her face.

Bill nodded in agreement. "Living things should always be treated with respect at the very least."

Leah laughed. "Harry is so different than my other horses, but that's what I like about him. Julie will take him if I kick the bucket or if anything happens to me. She'll take my dogs and cats too. She's the best."

Bill smiled. "It's good to plan for that sort of thing. You have dogs and cats too?"

Leah smiled. "Yes, I have two dogs and two cats." She shook her head. "I must be crazy, but I love them."

Bill looked at her. "That's nice. What do you mean that Harry is different?"

Leah just smiled. "He's his own person, for lack of a better expression." She kept thinking how easy it was to be around Bill. She nursed her wine. Bill finished his whiskey a while ago.

That made Bill laugh. "His own person. I see," he said.

Leah laughed. "This is such a nice party," Leah said to Bill.

Bill said softly, "Yes. Very. So tell me, what do you do for a living?"

Leah noticed that Bill didn't talk much about himself. She hoped it wasn't because she couldn't seem to be quiet. She was curious about him. "Believe it or not, I'm the office manager at a local animal rescue. I love it, but it's the hardest job I've ever had."

Bill smiled then laughed. "I, uh, I believe it. I'm sure it's very grueling. You know what, I'd love to meet Harry sometime if that would be all right."

Leah laughed. "Of course. I'd like that, and he'd like you, I'm sure." She finished her wine, looked up, and saw a lightning bug fly by the table. Without giving it a thought, Leah said, "Look, a lightning bug! I love them!" She couldn't seem to control herself. "Oh God, there I go again. I'm sorry," Leah said and rolled her eyes.

"You know what, so do I. Always have," Bill said. He smiled at her.

The way he looked at her, she knew he was enjoying her company. She felt relieved because she was afraid she sounded silly. "Really? Have you ever seen them in a field at night?" Leah asked.

"No," Bill said softly, "I can't say that I have."

"Oh, you have to! You wouldn't believe it. Would you like to go see what they look like?" Leah asked and wiped her mouth with her napkin.

Bill smiled, shrugged his shoulders, and said, "Sure. I'd love to. When?"

Leah stood up. "Now."

This made Bill laugh. "What?"

"Now. I know this field not far from here. Let's go." She stopped. "Oh, wait, I forgot, I don't have a car. I don't drive. I don't see very well, so I don't drive any longer. Julie brought me here tonight. She's a dream, you know. She brings me to work and home every day. I just love her. I knew it was time to hand in my keys the day I missed seeing a truck. How the hell do you miss seeing a truck?" Leah said and let out a sigh. "I've had vision problems for a while now. Really makes me mad and cramps my style."

Bill couldn't seem to resist how spontaneous she was. "I'll drive," Bill said and smiled.

Leah looked at him and smiled. She couldn't help but feel good about him.

Bill stood up and held out his hand to her. "Take my hand, so you don't fall."

"Oh, all right. Thank you," Leah said and smiled. She took his hand. His hand was so big compared to hers. It felt so comforting and safe. They walked toward the front.

"You really want to go?" Leah was surprised.

Bill smiled at her. "Yes, I do."

Julie was not far away, talking to some of her guests, when she saw them leaving and called to them, "Where are you two going?"

"To watch lightning bugs," Leah called back to her.

Julie whispered to herself, "What?" She looked puzzled, but smiled and shook her head and went back to her guests. As she mingled through the crowd, she passed Rob who was cleaning the grill. She stopped and whispered to him, "You won't believe this."

He smiled and said, "What won't I believe?"

"Leah just left with Bill, and I called to them to ask where they're going, and Leah yelled back, 'To watch lightning bugs.'"

Rob shook his head and laughed. "Okay."

Bill held the car door open for Leah. He then went to the driver's side and got in. "Okay, where do we go?" He said as he started the car.

"Down the street, out of this development. Turn left and keep going. You'll see it."

They pulled up to an abandoned lot with tall grass, trees, and bushes. "Now shut the car off and turn out the lights," Leah said.

Bill couldn't help himself. He laughed from deep down inside and said, "I'm sorry, Leah, but how do you know I'm not some crazy man? We've known each other for a few hours, and here we are alone on a dead-end road, and you tell me to shut the car off and turn out the lights."

Leah looked at Bill. "Okay, you have a point, but how do you know I'm not some crazy woman?" she said and began to laugh. "I never gave it a second thought, you being a crazy man, I mean. Julie wouldn't have anything to do with you if you weren't a good person. Plus, I see how Julie looks at you. You mean the world to her."

Bill smiled and looked at Leah. Their eyes met again. Leah loved his eyes. They smiled at each other. He shut the car off and turned out the lights. He looked at the field of lightning bugs. It was a light show to say the least. Every tree, blade of grass, and bush were lit with twinkling yellow lights. In a very soft voice, he said, "This is beautiful. I never would have thought—"

"I know," Leah said and smiled.

They sat for a while and watched the field light up. Neither said a word.

Bill's phone rang. "Hello. Oh, hi, Julie." He smiled. "Yes, watching lightning bugs," Bill said and laughed. Leah knew she was teasing him, and that she'd get it when they got back. "Dessert? Hold on," Bill turned to Leah. "Interested?"

"Of course. I'm hungry again," Leah said.

Bill laughed. "I swear, I don't know where you put it. Yes, Julie, we'll be back shortly. Thanks."

On the way back to Julie's, Leah looked at Bill. He struck her as strong and gentle. His eyes were soft, caring. Understanding and wonderful. She didn't understand how this could happen. She was calm, comfortable with Bill, and at the same time, panicked about feeling that way all at the same time.

They pulled up to Julie's. They could smell coffee in the air. Bill came to the passenger side of the car, opened the door for Leah, and took her hand to help her out.

"Thank you. It'd be pretty embarrassing if I fell flat on the ground," Leah said as she got out of the car. As they walked to the yard, Bill held her arm gently so she wouldn't stumble and fall.

Bill said. "I won't let you fall." He glanced at his watch and said, "It'll be late by the time we're finished. Can I take you home later?"

"Thank you, but I don't want to trouble you. Julie said she'd run me home."

"It's no trouble," Bill said.

Leah thought for a second. "All right. I'm sure Julie is getting tired and would like to relax." Leah smiled. "Thank you."

When Leah and Bill walked into the backyard, Leah was a little bit ahead of Bill. Julie came over to her, took her arm, and whispered in her ear, "Sure, lightning bugs!" They both laughed.

"Yes, watching lightning bugs. Bill was a perfect gentleman. Oh, before I forget," Leah said, "Bill said he'd take me home. So now you can relax and have that glass of wine you've been wanting."

"Great!" Julie said. Bill caught up to them just then. Julie smiled and said, "Come on, let's get some dessert."

It was well after midnight when people began to leave. Bill and Leah were walking around the yard admiring the flowers and landscaping. Leah noticed that Julie was beginning to clean up. "Bill, I'm going to help Julie clean up, okay?"

"Of course. I want to catch up with Rob anyway."

Rob was in the kitchen wrapping leftovers and having a cold beer. Bill walked in. "Let me give you a hand."

Rob smiled. "Hey, I was trying to catch up with you all night. What'll you have? Jack?"

"Yes, please," Bill said. Rob poured his drink. They tapped glasses. "You did a great job on dinner."

"I was taught by the best, Bill," Rob said. "And for that, I thank you. So, Bill, how's it going? Julie and I are so glad you came tonight."

Bill took another sip of his drink. "Things are going well. We miss you at the restaurant. If you ever give up on your construction business, please come back." Bill paused for a minute and said, "So I have a question for you."

"Sure, what?"

"Was this evening some sort of a setup? Were you two trying to play matchmaker with me and Leah?" Bill asked and took another sip of his drink and looked at Rob with a suspicious serious look.

"Oh boy, I was afraid you'd think that. No, Bill, it wasn't." Rob began to laugh. "Truth be told, Julie was trying to set Leah up with some guy who just wanted a casual relationship, someone to go to parties with, you know, just low key. This guy is a relative or something of one of her friends from the barn. Turns out, he changed his mind and didn't come. The seating arrangement got all messed up when Julie went to get Leah. They ran late. Your table was supposed to be full, with a sixth person, married and very happily I might add, but here alone because her husband is out of town. Apparently she caught up with another group of friends and sat with them."

Bill burst into laughter.

"It's the truth, Bill. It's just as well, though. Leah would have been mad as a hornet. She had no idea what Julie was planning. Julie is just trying to help her, that's all. And by the way, Leah cracked me up when she choked on your drink," Rob said.

Bill laughed and said, "You saw that?"

"Yup. Leah is strictly a wine person. When she gets real bold, she'll drink red. She must have been beyond bold at that moment." Rob just chuckled. Then he got serious. "Bill, I really wish you'd let me repay you. You know that if it weren't for you, we'd—"

Bill interrupted, "Stop, please. Your friendship is all the payback I need, If I remember correctly, you were there for me when I dropped out of life. You know what a dark place I was at in my life, and you and Julie were there for me. Tonight is the first time I'm actually enjoying myself in a social situation in a very long time. You and Julie welcomed me into your family. Nothing beats that."

Rob smiled. "You are family."

Bill laughed slightly. "Okay." And they raised their glasses to each other.

Rob asked Bill, "So given the turn of events, what do you think of Leah?"

"Oh, she's very nice. She makes me laugh. And wow, is she beautiful! I'm enjoying her company so much. She's so easy to be around. She's real if you know what I mean, and so spontaneous." Bill laughed slightly. "Which is nice. She's very open about the most interesting things." Bill smiled. "I'm glad Julie's little plot didn't work out after all. Tonight has been real nice."

Rob smiled. "Leah doesn't have an easy time being with people. She's not one to open up to a stranger. I'm surprised she even came tonight."

Bill looked at Rob and said, "I don't understand why she's alone. She should have a line of guys wanting to be with her."

Rob smiled a sad smile. He shook his head. "Let's just say life wasn't easy on her."

Bill sipped his drink. "She told me some things without telling me anything, if you know what I mean. She's a sweet girl. I'm having a very nice time with her."

Rob smiled. "I watched the two of you tonight, and she's having a nice time also, there's no doubt. This is a big move for her." Rob sipped his drink.

Just then, Julie and Leah walked in with more food. "Oh, here you two are," Julie said. "I'm glad you finally caught up. One more trip ought to do it, Leah," she said and they headed out again. "I'm so glad Bill is having a good time tonight," Julie said once they were outside. "He likes you very much."

"How can you tell?" Leah asked.

Julie laughed a little. "It's obvious, Leah. I've known Bill for a very long time, and the way he looks at you, well, let's just say I can tell."

"Julie, I'm scared to death. I really like him. I turned every thought and emotion off as far as having anyone being interested in me, let alone love me, or me love anyone else when I got sick years ago and ended up like I am. There's been nothing inside of me for so many years. I was hollow, dead inside. And now, I meet this guy, this guy Bill. I can't do this. I shouldn't do this, but I can't fight it. All the feelings I kept locked away are back. I don't want to lock them away again. A man could never and would never want to be with me. A monster wouldn't have me. What am I going to do? I know I just met him, but there's something about him." Leah fought back tears. She was so frustrated, so alone for so long.

Julie knew. "Listen, just enjoy him. You'll never meet a nicer man than Bill." She put her arm around Leah's shoulder.

Leah looked at Julie.

Julie, trying to avoid ruining the moment, said, "And don't start to cry. You'll ruin your face."

"Julie, I kept myself numb for so long. I'm afraid. Really afraid. Bill is so sweet, charming, he holds doors and even pulls my chair out for me to sit down. He holds my arm, so I don't fall and kill myself 'cause I'm blind as a bat. It doesn't even seem to faze him that I'm such a mess. He is so sweet. Julie, I've fallen for him, hard. I can't believe it. And, he's a lot of fun."

Julie got very serious and said, "He's been through hell, and I can see that you've fallen for him, and I think it's good for both of you. Let it happen. But," Julie smiled, paused, and then said, "Leah, he's a lot of man. So I have to ask you, will that bother you?"

Leah looked at Julie. She realized the depth of the friendship Julie and Rob had with Bill. "You're protecting him," Leah said and smiled. "But I think you know me better than that, Julie. I'm almost insulted."

Julie said, "I'm sorry, it's just—"

Leah interrupted her. "It's just beautiful to see this kind of friendship between people."

Julie smiled. "He's a very special part of our lives, Leah."

Leah could tell. She smiled. "Julie, when you walked me over to the table and introduced me to Bill, well, our eyes met and that was it. I couldn't hear or think. Everything around me stopped. Something happened right then and there. I felt human again. Everything I shut down came alive inside of me. But it's all wrong." Leah wanted to cry. She fought it. "He's a sweet, kind, gentle person. I'm so relaxed around him, and I don't understand it, but it's so nice. I had such a great time tonight. Who knew? He's so easy to be around. I'm so comfortable being with him. I know it sounds crazy, but it's true. And for the record," Leah paused and smiled, "I think he's very handsome."

Julie smiled. "We love him, Leah, we love him very much, that's all." Julie paused for a second. She smiled and said, "And like I said, I know he feels the same way about you."

"What, that I'm handsome?" Leah asked.

They both laughed and Julie said, "Oh shut up!" Then Julie got serious again. "So let me ask you this. Why is it so different in your mind for you?"

Leah got upset. "Not even close to the same thing. Leave me alone, Julie, just leave me alone."

"Okay, I'm sorry, Leah. I'm sorry," Julie said and put her hand on Leah's shoulder,

"Forget it. Just leave me the hell alone about things, okay?" Leah said.

Julie nodded.

Leah smiled. She didn't hold grudges, especially with Julie because she knows how much Julie cares about her. "It's fine. Forget it. I have a question for you, Julie. What is it that he did for you and Rob?"

Julie looked to make sure no one was close enough to hear them talking. "Well, years ago when we first got married, things were great. Rob's construction business was making money, I was working as a teacher, things were great. Then, of course, I got cancer, which, well, shot the budget to hell, and Rob's business began to fail. It was a hard time for a lot of businesses. He couldn't keep up with the pace. He was short help. He was trying his best to take care of me, pay the bills. The medical bills were outrageous. Both our parents had passed away early in our marriage, we're both only children, our families were small, everyone was gone by then, so we had no one to ask for help. It seemed like everything that could go wrong did. Our house was going to go into foreclosure. So we tried to save our credit by selling. One day we came home early, we misunderstood the realtor, and we showed up when he was showing Bill the house. At that time, Bill bought houses and fixed them up and resold them. I started to cry, I looked and felt like hell, bald as they come, skin and bones, and Rob lost it right in front of everyone. It was ugly. I never saw Rob like that. He was so angry and even very mean to Bill. I begged him to get back in the car and leave. He did, finally. Then, a few days later, the real estate agent calls us up and tells us that the house had been paid off in full. At first he wouldn't say how. Rob finally got it out of him that it was Bill. Bill got us back on our feet."

"Oh my God, really?" Leah whispered.

"Yes, and he would die first if he knew anyone knew. He'll deny it if anyone asks him about it. So you have no idea how kind this man is."

"How did he just pay it off like that?" Leah asked.

"He's pretty wealthy, another thing he'll never talk about. Unbelievable, isn't it?" Julie said.

In a quiet voice, Leah said, "Yeah, very. Okay, so how come I haven't met Bill until now?"

"That's a whole other story, and it's up to him to tell you. He left and went to California for a long time. Kept in touch for a while, then slacked off, and eventually no communication at all. We began to worry, Rob couldn't get in touch with him, so he went out and tracked him down. Long story short, he finally convinced Bill to come back."

"Oh boy, that sounds like something serious was going on," Leah said.

"To say the least, Leah," Julie said.

"Because of it all, or whatever, we all sort of adopted each other as family. He's the best friend Rob and I ever had. He's like a father to me. Bill is just Bill. A great guy."

"So how old is he anyway?" Leah asked.

Julie laughed. "Well, that's a random question. We're having a party for him at the end of September. He'll be sixty."

"So he's a little older than us, but not by much. Only ten years. Speaking of which, can you believe we're both fifty?" Leah said.

"Yes, I mean no. Half a century! Ouch!" Julie said. "We're past midlife unless we have magic genes."

"I'd like some magic jeans to make me look like a model or something," Leah said.

They both laughed.

"And what's so funny?" Rob said. He and Bill were standing behind them.

That just made them laugh even harder. "Oh, nothing. Just something about magic genes." Julie said.

"Bill, I think they're crazy. Let's go sit over there and talk," Rob said, and they walked to an empty table. Bill and Rob laughed as they walked away.

"Tonight was very nice, Rob, thanks," Bill said.

Rob just smiled.

Leah and Julie finished getting everything inside. The news on the TV announced that it was three thirty in the morning. Leah was surprised it was so late already. "Oh no, it's three thirty! And you still have the news on. Too funny. I hope Bill will still take me home." She walked over to Rob and Bill. "I'm sorry, Bill, but can you run me home?"

Bill looked at his watch. Surprised it was so late, he said, "Sure. Rob, again, thanks."

Julie walked over and said, "Bill, thanks for coming and taking Leah home."

Bill smiled. "The pleasure is all mine. I had a great time tonight. Thank you both. I'll be in touch." Bill got up, kissed Julie on the cheek, and took hold of Leah's arm very gently and said, as they walked to the car, "I don't want you to trip. It's pretty dark on the way to my car."

Julie looked at Rob as Bill and Leah walked away. "Do you see—"

Rob interrupted and said with a smile, "Oh yes."

Julie hugged Rob's waist. "Let's call it a day. I'm beat." They walked into the house holding each other.

On the way to her house, Leah looked at Bill and said, "I had a very nice time tonight. Sometimes, more often than not, I get so anxious in social situations. Most times, it gets out of control so I don't go to parties. Between that and the day I had, I almost didn't come tonight."

Bill laughed. "I'm right there with you. I'm not much of a social bug either. I don't get anxious, just don't seem to enjoy myself. I was this close to not accepting the invite tonight, but I'm glad I did. I had a very nice time also. Thank you for spending the evening with me."

Leah smiled at him. "My pleasure."

"Life can be a rough ride sometimes, if not most of the time," Bill said to her. By that remark, she knew he had been through it and back.

Leah smiled and nodded. They pulled up in front of her house. The porch light cast very interesting shadows on the lawn from all the flowers in her yard.

Bill looked at her. "Your yard is pretty. All wildflowers, right?"

"I love wildflowers." Leah said.

"They're very nice. They remind me of free spirits." Bill paused for a second, then said, "Would it be all right if I called you sometime soon?"

Her heart skipped a beat and she said, "I'd like that very much." She searched her purse for paper and a pen and finally found both. "This thing is a mess," she said. She wrote her number down and handed it to Bill.

Bill walked Leah to the door and stood with her while she unlocked it. He put his hand on her shoulder, smiled, and said, "Good night, Leah." Then he turned and walked to his car.

"'Night," she said and went in the house. She watched him from the window as he drove away. Her head was spinning. It was such a nice night. That scared her. Her dogs greeted her with wagging tails and happy barking. "Okay, I love you too!" Leah hugged and kissed them, took them out, and gave them something to eat. Her cats were already asleep on the couch for the night. She shook her head, smiled, and whispered, "Lazy bums."

She popped a piece of candy into her mouth, poured a glass of wine, put the TV on, turned all the lights off, and sat on the couch. The night allowed her to escape from herself, to not see herself, to be who she once was and longed to be again. It was a strange way to find peace, but it protected her from herself, and in the journey to sleep she was able to fantasize of who she wished she still was. The night was a dark, calm comfort that held her until morning.

"There's crazy stuff on at four in the morning," she said to herself. Leah drank her wine. Soon she was falling asleep on the couch. She couldn't get Bill off her mind. It was so out of character for her to say and do the things she did tonight. "God, I hope he calls me, and I hope he doesn't." She cried a little and fell fast asleep.

The sun woke her. Leah hated waking up each day. She looked around the room. Another night on the couch, the television still on. "I can't do this," she said out loud. "I just can't." She knew if she stayed on the couch for too long, it wouldn't be good. She'd feel worse than she did now. Ricky came over to her, wagging his tail, and he licked her face, as if to force her to get going with the day. He knew her very well. He loved her and watched her always. He always stuck close by Leah. Leah messed his hair and said softly, "My knight in shining armor." Honey seemed to hear her as she lay beside the couch. She looked at Ricky and wagged her tail.

Leah forced herself to get up and begin the day. She kissed Ricky on his forehead. Leah patted Honey and crawled off the couch. And so she began her awful morning routine. She always thought about ending it and wished she had the nerve. "I wish I didn't wake up. It was such a nice night last night, which is a perfect way to just go out and be done with it all. I wish I had the nerve to end it. The only thing stopping me is if I screw it up, then I'll have more crap to deal with. People thinking they know how I feel, deeming me crazy. Fuckers. Who the hell needs that? Someday I won't think about it, I'll just take my chances." She thought about Bill and began to cry.

Leah made some coffee. She took her time with it, enjoying every sip. Sunday was her least-favorite day. Too long and boring. Too much housework and yard work to do.

Finally the evening was near, and it was time for some dinner. Chinese takeout was always a great go-to. She ordered over the phone, and while she waited for delivery, she had some candy and poured a glass of wine for herself. She always gets dinner from the same place. The food was good, and there was always too much to finish, although she always did. She thought about Bill and how he laughed that she could eat so much. That made her smile. She thought to herself, *I'm in love with this man, and I hardly know him.*

She was sitting in the living room watching TV while she ate when the phone rang. Before answering, she drank some wine. "Hello?"

"Leah, hi. It's Julie. How are you?"

"I'm all right. Eating and drinking, watching television. Nothing exciting. What's going on?"

"Nothing. Just checking on you."

"Thanks. I'm fine. I can't believe you have that TV on, always listening to the news. I can hear it. If there was ever good news, I'd understand your craziness. What'd you do all day?"

Julie sighed and said, "The usual."

"Same here. Glad the day is over," Leah said.

"Me too. Thanks for coming last night," Julie said.

"It was a nice night. Bill asked for my number last night," Leah said, "but he hasn't called."

"Leah, it's only Sunday. He'll call if he asked for your number. You weren't even going to come last night, so relax."

Leah sighed. "Yeah, I guess you're right. It's just that, well, this is so crazy. I can't get involved with anyone, and yet I can't stop thinking about him. I just met him. I hardly know him, but I can't get him off my mind."

"Look," Julie said, "just relax and let things play out. He's a very nice guy. You're a very nice girl. Get some sleep. Are you working tomorrow?"

"No. I have the day off. Not sure what I'm going to do with myself," Leah said, and rolled her eyes.

Julie laughed. "Write a book."

Leah laughed. "Now that's a thought."

"Well, maybe Bill will call and take you somewhere," Julie said.

"Oh sure," Leah said, very sarcastically.

"Good night, you grumpy old woman. I'll call you tomorrow," Julie said and hung up.

It was going on eleven o'clock. Leah got comfortable on the couch. She put her phone down and shut her eyes. A few minutes later, her phone rang. Without looking to see who it was, she assumed it was Julie calling back to tell her something she heard on the news. "What'd you forget to tell me, Julie? Something on the news I should know?" Leah laughed.

There was a second of silence. "Leah, it's Bill. Is it too late to be calling? I wanted to call you earlier, but I got stuck at work."

Leah smiled. "Oh, Bill, hi. No, I'm just watching TV."

"I was calling to see if you're free tomorrow, or do you have to work?" Bill said.

"I have the day off," she said. Her heart began to race, and she was getting excited about seeing Bill.

"Can I pick you up sometime in the late afternoon? I thought we'd go to the country for a while and then to dinner, if that's all right."

"I'd love to," Leah said. She was so glad he called.

"Okay great! I'll see you around three?" Bill said.

"Perfect," Leah said.

"Good. I'll see you then," Bill said. He sounded happy.

Before he could hang up, Leah said, "Bill, thanks. It'll be fun."

"Yes, it will. Good night. See you tomorrow," he said softly and hung up.

Leah shut her eyes. *Oh boy*, she thought to herself.

Monday came quickly. Leah woke up on the couch. For a minute she felt disorientated. She thought for a minute, shook her head, and stood up. She looked out the window. It was a beautiful day. She felt that morning panic come over her again. She sat back down. She thought to herself, *I shouldn't be doing this with Bill.* At the same time, she couldn't wait to see him again.

Leah forced herself to get ready for the day. Soon she took a shower, refusing to look at herself. She'd mastered that after all this time. She had to fight off the thoughts of giving it all up. Those thoughts haunted her every day, oftentimes, all day.

Before long, it was almost three. Leah's stomach was in knots. She felt like a seventeen-year-old again. The doorbell rang. Leah looked out her bedroom window. Bill was on the porch.

Leah went downstairs. She opened the door and smiled. "Hi. C'mon in. Sit down," Leah said and motioned to the couch. "Can I get you anything?"

"No, thanks." He smiled. "It's such a beautiful day outside. Meant to be enjoyed. No lightning bugs, but a beautiful day nevertheless."

Her dogs came over to Bill happy to meet him. Bill smiled.

Leah tried to calm Ricky down. "This is Ricky. He loves people. And this is Honey. She has some issues as you can see." Her cats just slinked by, giving Bill the once-over. She laughed and said, "That means they approve."

"Oh," Bill said and laughed. "They're all beautiful," Bill said and rubbed Ricky and Honey between their ears. The cats were already sleeping in the sun under the living room window. "Where'd you get them?"

"I bought Ricky about ten years ago. I had always done independent rescue for years. All the dogs came with baggage of some sort, so I decided to buy a puppy and train him myself when my last rescue passed away." Leah laughed and said, "Some of my animals had so much baggage you wouldn't believe it. I was worn out. He's a bit spoiled, but a great dog. I got Honey from where I work. She came in as a stray and was up for adoption. She was up-front with us in the office because she didn't do well in the kennel for obvious reasons. I took a liking to her from the minute she hobbled down the hall. Turns out she has severe arthritis, which is obvious, Cushing's disease, Lyme disease, she is almost deaf and has cataracts. Poor thing, but she doesn't seem to know it, though, so no one tells her. I loved her so much. I decided to adopt her. Best decision I ever made. The cats were from a litter of a rescued pregnant cat. Chubbs is the oldest, and Huxley the youngest."

Bill smiled at her.

Leah smiled. "I'll be ready soon," Leah said and went back upstairs.

Bill sat on the couch. Ricky and Honey followed him and kept him company. Ricky jumped up and sat beside Bill. Honey lay down on the floor at Bill's feet. Both their tails were wagging.

When Leah came down the steps, she asked Bill, "Do I look all right?"

He stood up, smiled, and said, "You look great." Bill could see the doubt in her eyes. "You really do look great, Leah."

She hadn't noticed what he was wearing at first, but true to form, he was dressed very well. "You look very nice, too," Leah said.

Bill laughed. "Why thank you," he said and tilted his head. "You are too kind."

Leah smiled. "I mean it."

"Ready to go?" Bill asked.

"Yes," Leah said. "Where are we going?"

As they walked to the car, Bill told her, "I know a little piece of the countryside that is so peaceful and beautiful. I think you'll love it."

Bill was right. When they got into the country, the scenery was spectacular. Old houses, giant trees, rolling hills of nothing but green. The sky was a perfect blue. The air was so fresh it was hard to believe. Bill pulled the car over to a little spot on the side of the road. "Would you like to get out and take a walk?" he asked.

"I'd love to. This is so beautiful," Leah said.

There was a pathway that led into a wooded area. It was lined with wildflowers. It was getting late, and the shadows were changing. The sun that made it through the trees was so warm. They walked for a while in silence. Then Leah said quietly, "Look at all the wildflowers! They're so free, and quietly...wild."

Bill smiled at her. "After seeing your yard, the flowers are one reason I thought you might like it here." He looked at her and asked, "Can I hold your hand?"

"Yes, of course," she said, and he gently took hold of her hand as they walked. She felt safe holding his hand. "This reminds me of where I keep my horse. The barn is so peaceful, tucked away from all the craziness of this messed-up world. The silence and peacefulness comforts you, just like it's doing now. I always feel that I truly belong to this world when I'm there with my horse. I don't feel out of place."

"I know what you mean," Bill said quietly as they walked along. She believed he knew how she felt without knowing why. "So when we head back, we'll get some dinner. I know a terrific restaurant we can go to," Bill said.

"Sounds good. You know I'll be half-starved by then," Leah said.

Bill laughed. "Yes, I can only imagine."

They headed back to the car. "What a nice afternoon," Leah said.

"It was. Thanks for coming," Bill said. He started the car and rolled down the windows.

"Let me treat you to dinner, okay?" Leah said.

"No," Bill said.

"Okay, Dutch then," Leah said.

"Oh no, not with me. I asked you to join me," Bill said with a slight laugh in his voice.

Leah sighed. "Okay, so if I were to ask you to dinner, I can pay?"

Bill laughed. "You drive a hard bargain, you know?"

Leah just smiled.

Bill turned the radio on. Leah noticed he had satellite radio. As he went through the stations, she almost screamed, "Wait! Is that radio show *Gunsmoke*?"

Bill was surprised. "Yes, it is. You like that sort of thing?"

"Do I like it? I love it! Thank God for old-time radio! It brings back all the good stuff, and *Gunsmoke* is my favorite thing on earth. Matt Dillon is my hero!" Leah said and laughed.

Bill couldn't seem to stop laughing.

"What's so funny?" Leah asked.

"Oh, nothing. I just hadn't figured on you liking this. Especially radio. You're hardly old enough to even know *Gunsmoke* was on the radio."

Leah gave Bill a fake frown. "I'm not that young. I used to watch it on TV. I had no idea it started on radio. I heard it totally by accident one day on satellite radio in a friend's car. I was hooked right away. I fell in love with radio's Matt Dillon! And the love affair between Matt and Miss Kitty…the best and longest love affair of all time. I was so surprised to hear it! The whole thing is fascinating, and I like the radio show more than television because you get so caught up in it, and your imagination takes over and you get to create what the characters look like, the scenery, all of it. It's like you're right there in Dodge. My grandmother used to tell how much they loved the radio stories back in the day. Her face would light up when she talked about it. I knew she meant it, but couldn't imagine it. Now I know what she was talking about."

Bill laughed. He loved what she was saying.

Somehow Leah could tell Bill was wondering how old she was. "I'm fifty," she said.

Bill looked over at her. "Damn you're good!"

Leah smiled and settled back to listen to the radio. "I won't ask you," she said.

"I'm older than that," he said, and they listened to the story on the way to dinner.

"I'll bet you're turning sixty," Leah said with a smirk on her face.

"Like I said, you're good. How'd you know? A good guess?" Bill couldn't help but smile.

"Well, as much as I'd like to say I just knew, Julie told me."

"Oh…" Bill said and smiled. "Okay."

When they pulled up to the restaurant, Leah was surprised. It was very elegant to say the least. Bill got out and went to her side of the car to open the door. "Bill, this is one of the best restaurants in the country. I've read about this place. I've even seen it on television. Wait, do I look all right to go in?" Leah asked.

Bill winked at her. "You're fine." He took her hand to help her get out of the car.

Leah tended to forget that people couldn't see through her.

When they got to the door of the restaurant, Bill put his hand on her back to lead her in first. She couldn't believe how nice it was. She'd never go to a place like this on her own. She couldn't afford it. Bill noticed her looking around. "It's nice, isn't it?"

"Very," Leah said, almost in disbelief.

"I'd hoped you'd like it. I own this place," Bill said to her.

"Oh my goodness, you didn't tell me," she said.

"You didn't ask." He shook his head and chuckled.

"I used to be the chef here too. But I had to give that up. Too much standing. I can't do the physical work any longer. So I hired a wonderful chef who makes the most marvelous meals you've ever had. Rob used to work for me. We were sorry to see him go, but he had to move on. That's why he's such a great cook. He did very well for me."

"Oh," Leah said. "I knew he worked in a restaurant, but who knew?"

"We miss him," Bill said.

Leah kept looking around. "Bill, this is so, so like an old movie. A person would expect to see Bogie and Bacall here having dinner."

Bill smiled. "That was part of the idea. I guess it worked."

The hostess walked over. "Hello, Bill. We'll have your table ready soon."

Bill smiled. "Thanks. How is everything going tonight?"

"Things are going well," she said.

"Leah, this is Nancy, our hostess. Nancy, this is Leah, a friend of mine. We'll be in the bar. Just let me know when you're ready for us."

A few minutes later, a waiter came over to Nancy. He was young, with dark features, was tall and lanky, and had sort of a silly but very charming smile. He leaned close to Nancy and whispered, "Oh my God, Bill has a lady with him."

Nancy smiled. "Nick, I can see that."

"She's so pretty! I hope I have his table," he whispered.

Nancy shook her head in agreement. "Keep me posted on how it's going."

Bill pulled the chair out for Leah to sit down. The bartender came over. "Bill, how are you tonight?"

"Doing very well, thank you. Jess, I'd like you to meet Leah."

Jess reached over the bar and shook her hand. "What'll it be for you tonight, Leah?"

"Oh, a glass of white wine, dry please."

Bill said, "Our best, please."

Jess nodded. "Of course."

"And I'll have a Jack," Bill said. He turned to Leah. "I have to run to the kitchen for a second or two. I'll be right back, Leah."

"Sure," she said.

As she watched him walk away, she couldn't help thinking how nice he was, how she felt like she'd known him for so much longer than just three days. She loved how he dressed. So sharp, so precise. Leah hoped this would last, but knew in the end it couldn't be. It made her want to cry. She wished he'd kiss her. She wondered if he wanted to.

Bill came back, sipped his drink, and said, "I hope I wasn't too long. Just wanted to check on things."

Leah smiled. She was glad he was back. "No, you're fine."

Bill sat down and said, "Thank you for being my date today. And tonight."

"I really enjoyed myself today. You have to come meet my horse sometime soon."

Bill smiled. "I will, I promise."

Nancy came over to them. "Bill, your table is ready."

"Thank you." Bill stood up. He took Leah's hand so she could stand.

Leah smiled, almost laughing.

"What's funny?" Bill asked.

"Oh, nothing is funny. I think it's great that you have such wonderful manners," Leah said as they walked to the table.

"That's because I'm old," Bill said.

"You aren't old," Leah said. Leah just shook her head. "Whatever the reason, it's very nice." Of course, Bill pulled a chair out for Leah to sit down. She smiled. They looked at the menu, and Leah said, "I have a question."

Bill looked up at her.

"You and your staff are on a first-name basis?"

Bill smiled. "Yeah. I think when people work this hard, it makes it a little easier to be a little informal. I run a very tight ship, and they respect it. I respect them. We all work very hard to make this place work."

Leah smiled. "Makes sense."

Nick was their waiter. When he came over, he said, "Good evening, Bill. Good to see you."

"Hello, Nick. Nick, this is Leah. Leah, Nick," Bill said.

"Nice to meet you, Nick," Leah said. She finished the wine in her glass.

There was a bottle of wine on the table. Nick began to pour more in her glass. Leah smiled to thank him. "Bill, another Jack?"

"No, not right now, thanks. In a little while."

Suddenly, panic set in and Leah stood up. "I'm sorry, I have to run to the ladies' room for a second."

She began to shake. She stood in the stall. "Take a deep breath," she told herself. "Everything is fine. Now go back to the table and have a nice night." She took the ever-present bottle of water out of her purse, popped a piece of candy in her mouth, and took a sip of water.

When she stepped out of the stall, Nancy was standing by the mirror fixing her hair.

"Leah, hi!" Nancy said and fluffed her hair.

Leah returned the smile, hoping she didn't look panicked. "This is a great place."

Nancy nodded as she applied some lipstick. "Working for Bill is great. He's such a great guy."

Leah smiled and said, "I think so."

"I hope I'm not being nosey, but how did you two meet?" Nancy asked.

"At a party on Saturday. Actually, we were at Julie and Rob's. You know them. Bill told me Rob used to cook here," Leah said as she fixed her hair.

"Yeah, he was down on his luck, and Bill hired him and taught him how to cook. Bill does that a lot, hires people who are having a rough time."

Leah touched up her makeup. "Somehow, that doesn't surprise me."

"He's tough to work for, but fair. We all love and respect him. Few people that have worked here didn't work out. They were fools," Nancy said and finished fixing herself up. "Well, I have to get back to the floor. It was nice meeting you, Leah. Hope we'll see more of you."

"Same here, Nancy," Leah said and followed her out the door.

Leah sat back down. "So what will it be for you tonight?" Bill said. "Anything you want." Leah didn't know where to begin. She wasn't used to this type of life. Bill could tell. "Can I order for you? How about something with lobster and a bunch of wonderful things?"

Relieved, she said, "Please. That would be nice. I don't even know where to start." She smiled and said, "And I love lobster."

After Nick left the table with the order, Bill asked, "Is everything all right?"

Leah took a big sip of her wine. "Yes. I had to check my face, that's all."

Bill almost looked surprised. "Well, then you have nothing to worry about."

While they ate, Leah and Bill talked. She wanted to know all about him, but didn't want to appear as if she were prying.

Bill took a sip of his drink and said, "I can't help but notice how much of a lady you are. I noticed that at Julie's party. You carry yourself so well. It's nice to see that these days."

"Well, thank you, but I have my sixth-grade teacher to thank for that."

"Oh?" Bill said.

"Went to Catholic school for starters and had mostly nuns for teachers. My sixth-grade teacher was one of my favorites, but in the beginning, we were all scared to death of her. She had this reputation of being the meanest nun in the world. Turns out, she really cared about us. She was such a lady herself that she could peel and eat a grapefruit and not make a mess. I remember all of us watching her at lunch, the classroom was our lunchroom. We didn't have lunchrooms back then. Our parish was poor. My friends and I would wait for when she would get splashed with juice or something." Leah laughed. "It never happened. Beside all the lessons, she was determined to make ladies and gentlemen out of us. She would stop in the middle of a lesson, tell us to close our books, stand up, and show her our hands. God forbid your nails were dirty and not groomed!"

Bill looked at his hands. He sighed a sigh of relief.

"Yes," Leah said, "I noticed how well you take care of yourself." Bill laughed, and made a face of relief.

Leah had to laugh also. "Then, every Friday afternoon, all the girls in the sixth grade came to our room, the boys went to the other sixth-grade teacher. He was a man. Anyway, our teacher would make us put a book on our head and walk through the whole building until we could go all the way without dropping the book and our feet were not making any noise. It was a three-story building with lots of stairs. She'd say, 'Ladies don't make noise when they walk.' And believe me, we didn't make noise when we walked. Thank God for her. She taught us so much more than our ABC's."

Bill laughed right out loud. "Well, it paid off, Leah. I'm proud to have you with me."

Leah just smiled. He made her feel so good. She couldn't understand how or why. She felt good was all she knew. That scared her and made her feel wonderful all at the same time.

Nick walked over to Nancy and whispered, "Look at them. Bill looks so different tonight. He looks—"

"Happy," Nancy said. "For the first time since I've worked here."

On the way home, Leah felt much more relaxed. Bill had the radio on low. "I looked for *Gunsmoke*, but it's not on the schedule for tonight."

Leah laughed. "You did? How?"

Bill smiled and said, "I looked it up on my computer in my office when I went to the kitchen."

Leah smiled and said, "That so sweet."

Kidding, Bill said, "I'm just so sweet."

Leah said, "Yes, you are. And I had such a nice time today, Bill. Thank you."

Bill scrolled through the stations. "You're more than welcome, Leah."

"This Guy's in Love with You" by Herb Alpert had just begun to play. Just before Bill changed the station, Leah said, "I love that song! Leave it on, please! I bought that song, on a 45, when I was eleven. I thought, way back then, and still do, that it's the best love song ever. It still gives me chills when I hear it, all these years later. I can remember thinking every time I heard it how wonderful it would be for a girl to have a guy feel that way about her. Can I listen?" Then she realized she must have sounded so silly. "I'm sorry. I must sound like a fool."

Bill smiled. He so enjoyed the things she'd say. "Not at all. You sound like a romantic. And of course, you can listen," he said and let it play. They were quiet as the song played. He glanced over at Leah and could see how much she loved that song. That made him smile. When it finished playing, he said, "I had a very nice time today, Leah." As they pulled up in front of Leah's house, Bill asked, "Can I call you again?"

Leah nodded. "I'd like that." She smiled.

He walked her to the door and waited until she unlocked and opened the door. She began to walk inside. "Leah," Bill said, and he held her shoulder. He leaned over and kissed her on her cheek. "Good night." He turned to leave.

Before Leah went inside, she said, "Good night." She went inside and started to close the door, but she turned and said, "Bill,"

He turned to her. "Yes?"

Leah went over to him and returned the kiss on his cheek. He watched her walk inside and close the door. He smiled.

Leah had to work the next day. She had a hard time falling asleep. Her head was spinning, her heart was confused, and she was worried sick. She knew this man for three days, and she couldn't stop thinking about him. She wondered if he felt the same. She hoped he did. She could see he did. She was afraid he did.

It was a busy day at work for Leah. She was in her office trying to get some paperwork finished and was struggling to concentrate. She couldn't stop thinking about Bill. The phones didn't stop, people walking in all day with issues, good and bad, but all involving their animals. Leah took her job home with her every day. As she sat at her desk, papers everywhere, she just shook her head and said out loud, "I don't even know where to begin."

"Well, how about you start by coming up front?" someone said from the door.

Leah turned around. Her assistant was standing at the doorway. "There's some guy here who wants to see you," she said.

"Some guy? Who? And what does he want, Macie?" Leah asked.

She shrugged her shoulders. "I don't know. He just asked to see you."

Leah smiled, "Okay. I'm coming," she said as she walked down the hall. "Let him know I'll be right there. It's probably someone wanting to surrender twenty-five large dogs and five mean cats. I give up." When Leah walked to the front, she was surprised to see Bill standing there. She smiled. "Oh, you heard that."

He smiled and said, "Yes, I heard that. I only have twenty large dogs and three mean cats."

"Not funny!" Leah said.

They both laughed and Bill said, "I'm sorry to bother you at work, but I thought you might need this today," and he handed Leah her wallet. "It was on the floor of my car. Must have fallen out of your purse at some point."

Leah smiled and said, "Oh my. I never even missed it. Thanks! I would have died if I had looked for it and not found it. And you're not bothering me at work, Bill. Thank you so much." She was so glad to see him. "Can you stay for a minute?"

"Sure," he said. "I have to get back to work, but I have some time."

"Great. Come on back," Leah motioned for him to follow her. "This is my office. Look at this mess. So much paperwork! Sit down for a second."

"This is a nice office. Paperwork is stressful, I'll give you that," Bill said.

Leah rolled her eyes. "Yeah, a little. Can I give you my work number?"

"Yes, please," Bill answered.

She handed him her card. "Call sometime. I always need a sane person to talk to."

He laughed. "Well, I'm not sure that I'm the one for that, but I'll call."

Leah laughed. "Would you like some coffee? I need some real bad."

Bill looked at his watch. "Sure, I have time for a cup. That'd be great."

She poured two cups. She took some cream out of the fridge in her office. "Sugar, black, sweetener? How do you like it?" Leah said as she made hers.

Bill watched. "Same. Cream and sweetener please."

They chatted for about half an hour. Leah told him about her job, how sometimes—many times—she lost sleep over it. "It's also so nice that Julie brings me in and takes me home. My vision is so bad. I told you the night we met that I have vision problems. I actually went blind in my right eye a few years back. Julie can tell you. My macula and retina both detached."

"What?" Bill was very surprised.

"Oh yeah. Scary! Had surgery and everything. And the best black eye anyone ever saw. That's why one eye is a little bigger than the other. Another great feature of mine."

Bill had to smile, but inside he knew she had issues with her appearance. He got serious for a second. "Leah, I didn't notice." He sipped his coffee. "Mmm, this is perfect. I can't imagine you with a black eye. You know, there is nothing wrong with your looks. Believe me."

"Well, thank you, but you lie," Leah said and laughed. "Anyway, thank God for modern medicine. I can't see well out of that eye, but at least I can see."

"I'm glad things worked out for you. That's a pretty scary thing to go through," Bill said as he finished his coffee.

Leah smiled and finished her coffee. "Yeah, but I survived. My other eye isn't so great either. Detached retina and never the same since. Old age is taking over. Oh well, could be worse, I guess."

"This is all pretty serious. You handle it well," Bill said and smiled.

"What choice do I have?" Leah said and shrugged. "I have a great backup, Julie and Rob."

"I know you appreciate them. They're good people, no doubt. The coffee was just what I needed. I do have to go, but I'll be in touch, okay?" Bill said.

"I'll walk you to your car if that's all right," Leah said.

"Of course." He stepped aside to let her go first.

Leah giggled. She loved his manners. They walked to his car. "You know, I had such a nice time yesterday. Thank you so much. And your restaurant is wonderful."

Bill smiled at her. Leah felt like a kid. Bill could tell. It made him feel good. He leaned over and kissed her forehead. "I'll call you, and maybe we can make a date so I can meet Harry."

"Of course," Leah said, wanting to say, "How about right now?" She knew she had fallen deeply in love with this wonderful man, and she couldn't seem to help herself.

When Leah came back in the office, Macie just looked at her. She smiled. "So, you just lit up like a Christmas tree when you saw him."

Leah didn't answer her. She just walked back to the office, with a big smile on her face. She called back to Macie. "We met on Saturday at a party."

Leah sat down and didn't realize Macie had followed her back. "And so did he."

She was startled as she turned to see Macie standing there. "And so did he what?" Leah said, laughing at herself.

"Lit up like a Christmas tree when he saw you," Macie said and winked at Leah. Macie laughed. "And he's adorable, you know," she said, as she turned and walked back up front.

Leah smiled and called back to her, "I know."

Macie and Leah were good friends. Macie was considerably older than Leah, but they had so many things in common, except that Leah worked for the money, and Macie worked to get out of the house. She wasn't the retiring type. Macie even had a horse for twenty-five years. They had many heart-to-heart talks, and Leah trusted her enough to confide most things to her. Leah hadn't really had a chance to tell her about the weekend and how suddenly she was thrust into this crazy some kind of love affair that wasn't yet, but she hoped and at the same time she was scared to death that it would be. "Lunch tomorrow so we can talk," Macie yelled back.

"Of course. I can't wait to tell you all about him," Leah said.

"I can't wait to hear all about him," Macie said as she went back up front.

The next day turned out to be a slow day at the rescue, which enabled Macie and Leah time to talk and have lunch together. That was a rare moment on any given day. They ordered a pizza and ate at their desks.

"Okay, missy, spill it," Macie said.

A huge smile came to Leah's face. "Well, you won't believe it. I was invited to this party that my best friend, Julie, the girl who takes me to and from work, was having. I, of course, didn't want to go. I was so close to not going."

"Big surprise," Macie said and took a big bite of her pizza.

"Well, we got there late because of me, and she seats me at this table with five people. All couples except for this one man. His name is Bill. Well, what choice do I have? Julie introduces us, and our eyes met. Macie, it was amazing. Turns out, this man is a dream. He's like out of an old movie. So polite. He stands up, pulls the chair out for me so I can sit down, I couldn't believe it. Then, to top it off, I feel like I've known him forever. He is so easy to get along with. So comfortable. I said and did things I'd never do." Leah took a bite of her pizza and said, "You won't believe this."

"What? You sound so surprised at yourself." This made Macie laugh.

"Well, I am. I took a drink of his whiskey right out of his glass, damn near choked and died."

"What? You did what? You who won't let anyone touch your food or..." Macie just stared at her.

Leah had to laugh and interrupted, "I told you, you wouldn't believe it. Then."

"Oh no, then what? Can I stand it?" Macie asked, laughing.

"I don't know. I asked Bill what this food was on his plate, because I missed it at the buffet table. I had my plate full to the breaking point, which was amusing to him—"

Macie interrupted. "Well, of course it was. Look at you. You're this little bitty thing. I still can't believe what you can put away. If I hadn't seen you eat when we went out, I'd swear you don't eat at all. So you didn't take it off his plate," and in a quiet whisper, Macie continued, "did you?"

"Yes, yes I did!" Leah said and burst out laughing. "Then, as we're sitting there, this lightning bug flies by, and I blurt out, 'A lightning bug. I love them!' I had no filter, Macie. I couldn't control myself. It felt so good. Then, I asked Bill if he'd ever seen them in a dark field, he said no, and then I asked him if he'd like to go see lightning bugs in a dark field, he said yes, and we went to an abandoned lot to look at lightning bugs. He asked me what if he was some sort of crazy man. I said I knew he wasn't, and I could be a crazy woman for all he knew. Macie, he is so…so…something. I can't describe it."

"You sound like a seventeen-year-old schoolgirl, Leah." Macie said and laughed.

"That's exactly how I feel. And I love it. I love him. I know how crazy it is, but sometimes you just know. And I'm scared to death. This whole thing scares me to death."

"I'm happy for you. He sounds wonderful, Leah," Macie said and chuckled. "Don't be scared. Be happy." Macie didn't know Leah's issues. That was the one thing Leah couldn't talk about.

The phone rang. Leah looked at Macie and said. "How rude, we're trying to have a conversation." They both laughed. Leah answered the phone, and at the same time, a customer came in. Lunch was over.

Julie came to get Leah after work. Leah was so grateful for the continuing favor. When Leah got in the car, she looked tired. Julie asked, "Crazy day?"

"Not more than usual," Leah said. "I do have a question for you, though."

"What?" Julie asked.

"Was Saturday a setup? You know, for me to meet Bill? I was telling my friend at work about Saturday, and suddenly I realized it could have very well been a setup."

Julie laughed. "Bill asked Rob the same thing on Saturday when they were talking in the kitchen. Well, I mean, no, not to set you up with Bill. One of our riding buddies asked me if their cousin or some kind of relative could come and meet you. He wanted a no-strings-attached, very casual relationship. He changed his mind about coming last minute, and I had you seated with the girls you had those Thursday-night lessons with, you know, the lessons when you'd all just sit around on your horses talking? Best lessons those horses ever had. Anyway, by the time we got to the party, that went to hell in a handbasket. The seat at Bill's table was open because a girl whose husband was out of town caught up with friends, and sat with them instead.'"

Leah just stared at Julie. Then she began to laugh. "Un-fucking real! I'm glad he didn't show. He was probably some kind of a creep from under a rock. Don't ever to that to me again, Julie."

Julie had to laugh. "I know, I'm sorry. I'll never do that to you again, I promise. I just thought it would get you to come out more, I'm sorry."

Leah shook her head. "You are a sick individual, do you know that? But I love you."

When Leah walked in the door, Ricky and Honey ran up to her and greeted her with wagging tails and kisses. "I love you two so much!" Her phone rang. "Hello?" she said.

"Hi, Leah. It's me," Bill said. "I have a question. Can I pick you up after work tomorrow, and can I meet Harry? Then we can grab some dinner."

Leah was so glad to hear from him. "Sure. We can get take out and come back here if that's okay."

"Sure, that'd be nice. What time do you get off work?" he asked.

"Seven. We'll end up eating late, is that okay?" Leah asked.

Bill laughed. "Leah, I have my restaurant. Dinner is never before nine for me."

"Can't wait for you to meet Harry. You'll love him. Oh, and I'm buying dinner," Leah said.

Bill laughed out loud. "Okay, fine. See you at seven tomorrow. Good night now."

The next day, Leah couldn't wait to get off work. The day seemed like a month of Sundays.

Macie noticed how antsy Leah was all day. Her fuse was shorter than normal.

"Leah," Macie said, "what's gotten into you today?"

"I'm sorry. Bill is coming to get me from work, and I just can't wait. We're going to see Harry then get dinner. I just can't wait to be with him, Macie."

Macie smiled at her. "You're lucky, you know."

Leah nodded.

Finally, seven o'clock rolled around. Of course, customers were still at the shelter. That was just how it was. Leah was taking care of a woman who just adopted a dog and was making her donation to pay for him. She looked up from her computer, and Bill was standing by the wall behind the crowd. She smiled.

Leah finished up with the woman in about fifteen minutes. Some of the younger kids (Macie and Leah always called the employees under forty kids), who worked at the shelter came up front to say goodbye to the dog and celebrate the adoption as was the custom.

Macie looked at Leah. "Go. Get out of here. I'll close up."

Leah looked so happy to be able to go. "Thank you! You are a saint!" She shut her computer off, and walked over to Bill.

"Ready?" Bill asked.

"Very," she said.

He put his arm around her waist, and they walked out.

One of the kids, Kallie, who was very outgoing, easygoing, and a great comedienne looked at Macie and said, "Okay then... Wow! I had no idea." She winked at Macie and said, "I'm going to tease her tomorrow. Can't wait!"

This broke Macie up. She couldn't stop laughing.

They laughed a lot at the shelter. They had to keep their sense of humor in the day to keep the stress level down to where they could handle it. Everyone at the shelter worked as a team and helped each other always. They all worked hard, and the animals always came first.

As they walked to Bill's car, Leah said, "I can't wait for you to meet Harry."

"I don't know a thing about horses, Leah," Bill said.

She could tell by the look on Bill's face and the tone of his voice that he was nervous. "There's nothing to it. You'll be fine. I'm glad it's light late now. I love the longer days."

They pulled up to the barn. Leah pulled a bag of watermelon that she had cut into pieces from her purse for Harry.

"This is nice," Bill said. "Like a trip back in time."

"I love it. This barn must be at least two hundred years old. Look at the landscape. Harry is out in that field, just beyond the barn," Leah said. Her eyes lit up.

Bill could tell how much she loved her horse. He knew from the look on her face that this was her escape. As they walked to the field, Bill held her hand.

When they got to the gate, Leah said, "Wait here. I forgot to get his brush out of the barn. Stay here and just watch for a second." When she came back, she walked into the field and called Harry. He came running in. He stopped at her feet and put his lips on her cheek. She gave him a piece of watermelon.

"Oh my God," Bill said. "That was so beautiful!"

Leah smiled. "Come in and meet him, Bill," Leah said. She began to brush him.

Bill began to pet him. "Can I brush him?"

"Sure. Here." She handed him the brush and said, "Just go in circles." Leah combed Harry's mane and tail.

Bill seemed to like it. Suddenly, Harry turned his face to Bill and kissed him on his cheek. Leah quickly handed him a piece of watermelon. "Give this to him, "Leah said. "You'll be best friends."

Bill couldn't help but smile. "This is so nice, so peaceful."

Leah laughed. "This is my haven. No one and nothing can get me here. Not even myself," she said.

Bill looked at her. Not understanding her last remark, but knowing it was true for her. He somehow understood Leah without understanding her at all. What he did understand was he, too, had fallen deeply in love with her and he hoped that she knew it.

"Let's hand-graze Harry," Leah said.

"Not sure what that is," Bill said and laughed. "I told you, I know nothing about horses."

Leah looked at him and had a funny smile on her face,

"Oh no," Bill said. "I think that means I'm going to learn." And he laughed.

"You got it, mister. You'll love it. Horses are really peaceful, you know."

Bill could tell she meant it and that Harry was her peace.

Leah put Harry's halter on. "Did you see that?" she asked.

"Uh, yeah, I guess so," Bill said.

"Okay, watch again." She took his halter off, and put it on again. "Well?"

"I got it this time," Bill said, afraid to say otherwise. She knew that and laughed.

"You attach the lead to this little round circle clip down here, then just walk him out of the field, to the grass, and let him eat." Leah gave Bill a look that made him laugh.

"Okay, I got it," Bill said.

"Here, take the lead and let Harry eat," Leah said and handed Bill the lead.

"What if he…" Bill said, looking frightened.

"He won't, don't worry. I promise," Leah said. "He loves this. The problem you'll have is getting him back in the field."

Bill stared at her. "Oh no…"

Leah laughed. "I'll help you." She laughed and rubbed Bill's shoulder.

As they stood and let Harry graze, Bill said to Leah. "We've had so many conversations, but you never speak of your parents or background. Can I ask why?" The way she looked at Bill told him she was not comfortable with this. "Oh, I'm sorry. I didn't mean to—"

"Don't worry. I never talk about that. It's not a pleasant subject in my life. I always wondered about myself, you know, how I've done in life. And then, just in recent years, when I met up with people who knew me growing up, told me they are impressed at how I managed to land on my feet. Relatives and friends always told me that I did exceptionally well, considering what I was up against. Makes me feel better about myself to hear things like that. God, it was rough."

Bill just stared at her. "I'm sorry," he said.

"Don't be. My parents had some bad times and I guess got caught up in it all. One day, when I was fifteen, in ninth grade, I came home from school and a note was on the fridge from my mother saying she left, blaming my father for everything. Both were at fault. No one knew where she had gone. How do you think something like that makes a kid feel? So I acted like I didn't care. This was close to finals in ninth grade. I took over the house, cleaning, cooking, trying to take care of my dad. I did the best I could at that age. One day, at school, I went to the nurse. I just felt tired, or something like that. Deserted I guess, worthless. There's that worthless thing again. Anyway, I told her I had a headache. She asked me about home. Very nonchalant I told her what happened, and I said something like I was a little upset over it. I wasn't crying or anything. She looked at me like no one ever had, and I realized she was extremely surprised. She said I was in no condition to take finals. I felt so relieved because that was really causing me stress since concentrating wasn't exactly something I was doing very well at the time. Spent most of my time burying my feelings as deep as I possibly could. I couldn't understand how this perfect stranger, the school nurse, summed it up. I could tell by the look on her face that she knew exactly what was going on inside of me. Then, my social studies teacher, who was so gruff and nonreactive—or so it seemed, and I thought he hated me and all his students—came to me at the end of class one day and said how sorry he was about what I was going through and that he hoped I was okay. Unreal. One of my first real-life lessons, never judge what appears to be. Wait and see what it really is.

I'd cook for my father. He had a girlfriend, who came first, always. Nothing mattered but her. A few years later, he loses the house. Talk about getting hit from behind by a bus. He rents this apartment down the street. To make it stay as much the same as possible. So I go to the house one day and ask the landlord if I can go in and see my room. She looked at me like I had three heads and said, "It's just your father. No one else." I had no idea. I remember just standing there, like I was nothing. I think that was the moment I really believed I was nothing. Twice I was dumped, once by each of my parents. So I just walked away. I had a dog and nowhere to go. Just like that. I have no love loss for them, believe me. I'm almost ashamed to say that, but it's the truth. I don't hate them, I'm just very disappointed and hurt, mostly hurt. It hurts too much. Anyway, when I confronted him about this, he just walked away. I was dismissed like yesterday's news. Luckily a good friend at the time helped me with my dog, so at least that part turned out all right. I'm sorry, but I don't want to talk about it anymore."

Bill held her hand and looked at her. "I understand."

Leah just smiled. She knew she was lucky to have a man like Bill.

Bill looked at her and said, "I guess you want to know about my past."

"If you want to talk about it," she said.

"Fair enough." Bill gave Harry a pat on his neck. "My dad passed away when I was sixteen. My mother was very abusive to us. Punishment was a beating and/or being locked in a closet, among other things. It wasn't an easy life. To this day I can't talk about all of it, but I made it through, worked hard to get where I am. Then life became good. I feel like I'm a successful person. Not very interesting, but that's basically it in a nutshell."

She said in a quiet whisper, "So we both came through it and landed on our feet."

Bill looked at Leah, smiled at her, looked into her eyes, and said, "Yeah."

"You know what, I wish we could go riding into the sunset and never come back," Leah said as she put her arm around Harry's neck and kissed him.

Bill smiled. "If you can find a horse who can carry me, I'd love to. I wish I were—"

"I don't," Leah interrupted. "You're perfect. We can hand-graze all the way outta here. Just the three of us," Leah said to Bill, and hugged him. She reached up and kissed his cheek. He smiled and ran his hands through her hair and kissed her forehead.

When Leah got to work the next day, all the "kids" were waiting for her at the front desk. She looked at them and said, "What the hell is going on?"

They burst into laughter. Kallie, the young woman who promised to tease her, said, "You are in love, and so is he. And he's cute too!"

Leah just looked at them. She had to laugh. "Is it that obvious?"

All at once, they all said, "Very!"

Leah's face turned beet red, and she went to her office. As she walked down the hall, she yelled, "You're a bunch of crazy people. I love you!" They all laughed. So did Leah.

Bill and Leah had been dating for a while now. They knew they were in love; both of them knew the other was the one. Leah loved Bill deeply. It frightened her because their feelings for each other were so strong. She began to feel that strong panic, along with the depression she couldn't seem to escape, creeping into her. It was taking over her again.

# CHAPTER 2

## *Hurting and Loving*

It was a Tuesday morning. Leah woke up feeling totally consumed by her depression. The roller-coaster ride with her issues was exhausting. Leah called out of work, and she told Julie she wasn't well and wouldn't be going to work. Wednesday came, and she took off. She never called Julie, and by late Thursday, Julie panicked. She knew Leah struggled with depression. She knew it would come on at any time. In an instant it would incapacitate her.

Leah had continually asked her not to discuss her issues, so Julie couldn't confide in anyone. It frightened Julie that she hadn't heard from Leah. She called Bill to see if he had heard from her.

"No, I haven't heard from her. I called her a few times over the last few days and got nothing. I'm thinking she thought it over, you know, about us, and decided she isn't interested. Can't say that I blame her. I expected this. I really did." Bill had a sadness in his voice.

"Bill, it isn't what you think," Julie said. "She's in trouble. Leah has severe depression issues. I shouldn't be telling you, but you need to know. I'm afraid. Will you meet me and Rob at her house?"

"I'll be there," he said.

"Good. I have a key, so if we get there before you, just come in," Julie said and hung up.

Julie, Rob, and Bill arrived at Leah's at the same time. They rushed in. No sign of her. The bedroom door was closed. Ricky was lying by it. Honey, too old to climb the stairs, stayed at the bottom

54

and barked. Julie ran to the bedroom. Leah was lying across the bed asleep. Julie saw a pill bottle and an empty bottle of wine beside a wineglass on the night table. "Leah, oh my God! Get up!" Julie yelled. She shook her. Bill and Rob came in.

Bill just stared at her. He moved Julie out of the way and lifted Leah up off the pillow. He shouted, "Leah! Wake up!" He got very loud and profound. "Damn it! I said wake up!"

Leah opened her eyes. She just looked at him. She began to cry.

Bill sat on the side of her bed and pulled her close to him. He held her head on his chest and rocked her in his arms. "Leah, oh my God, Leah."

She whispered, "I want to be numb, not feel who I am. I guess I took too many pills and had too much wine. I just want to die. I don't want to feel anything anymore. It hurts too much. Oh God, I can't take it anymore. I'm finished. So finished. You could never understand."

Bill continued to rock her. He ran his hands through her soft hair. "Sweetheart." He paused and took a deep breath. "Leah, I thought things were going so well between us. I can't go through this a second time, losing someone I love more than life. I just can't. I can't do it."

Julie and Rob, relieved she was all right, just held each other.

Leah looked at Bill. His eyes were so sad. Julie and Rob looked at Leah. They knew what Bill was about to tell Leah. They left the room.

Leah said to Bill, "You can't love me, Bill. Even if you think you do."

"You know I do. How can you not see that?" Bill continued to hold her.

"What do you mean you can't go through this a second time?" Leah was confused for a second, then realized this must be what Julie meant when she said he'd have to tell her about this part of his life.

Bill began to tell Leah, "I was married. I lost my wife to cancer years ago. She was the love of my life." His eyes had a distant look.

"Oh, Bill, I'm so sorry," Leah said, still crying.

"Thing is, I still love her. I can't erase what we had. Can you understand that?"

Leah looked at Bill. This was not what she expected, but was glad to know. She paused, got her thoughts together, wiped her eyes, and said, "Of course. You should always love her, Bill. Always keep her in your heart. She must have been one hell of a woman for you to love her like this. She will always be a part of your life and always should be."

Bill didn't expect that for an answer, but he took her hand and said, "You are something very special. Can you understand that I also love you? Very much?" He was fighting back tears, but one rolled down his cheek.

Leah took her hand and wiped the tear off his face. "Yes, I do, Bill."

Bill put his arm around her. "I love you, Leah. I really do love you," he said softly.

Leah knew he did, and she realized how lucky she was, but was still so afraid that in the end, it wouldn't be possible.

Bill smiled and continued to tell her, "I met Julie and Rob when, well, when they were having a hard time. I'm sure you know about Julie's cancer." Leah nodded. "I bought their house back for them when they were about to lose it. I knew what they were going through, and I knew we, my wife and I, were lucky enough not to have any financial problems." Bill stopped for a second. He half-smiled. "She told you about the house and how we first met, didn't she?"

Leah nodded and whispered, "You're not mad at her? Are you?"

"No, of course not. Did she tell you I was married?"

"No, she didn't. She said there was a private part of your life, and it was up to you to let me know or not."

"My wife and I made it through that nightmare. My wife beat the cancer the first time. We hoped against hope that it wouldn't return. I wanted to give Rob and Julie the same chance that we were given, the chance to be happy and live a normal life. I knew how much they loved each other. You could see it. Rob totally lost control and some of the things he said, well, I knew then how badly he was hurting inside. It's funny, but if you watch close, and listen, you can see there's more to it than meets the eye. It wasn't right that we could make it, and they couldn't. I couldn't take their house and their livelihood away from them. A few years later, my wife's cancer came back with a vengeance and took her from me. I lost it. I just couldn't cope any longer. I kept in touch with Rob and Julie, and even my in-laws for a while, but it hurt too much. I got to a very low point in my life, and I just stopped. I stopped everything."

Leah felt so terrible for him. The tears flowed uncontrollably. She didn't know what to say. His pain was so intense that she could feel it. He never made an attempt to touch her except for a kiss on her cheek, holding her hand and a gentle kiss on the lips. She wondered if it was because of the love he still had for his wife. And that was all right with her. She thought for a second and said, "Bill, why don't you call or see your in-laws? I'll bet they would love to hear from you."

He looked at her and didn't say a word. He just nodded and shrugged his shoulders. He held her tight. "After I lost my wife, I died inside. I thought I'd never be able to love anyone again. I stayed to myself. I only did what I had to do to survive." Bill stopped for a second. He smiled, but it was a sad smile. "I was so different back then. Young, and in shape. My wife always told me how proud she was to be with me." He sighed. "Oh well, food became and is my comfort I guess, with a drink here and there, many times very here and there. What can I say? I accept myself. I was so dead inside for so long, I just didn't care, and then, well, when I met you, it was love at first sight, at least for me. The whole thing is as if I was under some sort of spell. I saw you and just felt so at ease being with you, talking to you, you made me laugh so much."

She broke away from his hold. Leah just looked at him. Their eyes locked. "Love at first sight? Oh my God, that's exactly how I felt. It felt like—"

Bill finished her sentence, "Time stood still and this calm, quiet feeling came over me."

She just stared at him in disbelief. They both smiled. There was a long silence, a positive silence, securing this bond between them.

Leah was trying to process all she had heard and all she was feeling, all the feelings within herself and what Bill was sharing with her.

She put her hand on his shoulder. "Bill, I'm very proud to be with you, and don't you ever think I'm not." She leaned toward him and kissed his lips. He put his arms around her.

She felt so thin to his touch. Bill took a tissue from the night table and handed it to Leah to wipe her face. "When was the last time you ate? You feel so thin. You can't afford to lose any weight. You're scaring me, Leah."

She shrugged her shoulders. "I don't know. Three days maybe. I can't eat when I get like this."

"C'mon, get up and I'll make something for you, or get something, whatever you want. Not that it's any of my business, but what about work?"

"Macie has me covered. She's a good friend, and she's handling things for me."

Bill held Leah's hands. "Good, 'cause you're taking tomorrow off to rest.

Julie and Rob knocked. Julie said, "Can we come in?"

"Yes," Leah said.

Bill turned to them. She needs something to eat. "Hasn't eaten in days." He shook his head and hugged her.

Leah began to cry again.

"Leah," Bill said, "what—"

She interrupted. "I'm sorry. Just can't stop crying."

"She's a cryer, Bill. Cries over everything." Julie smiled. "Leah," Julie said, "get up, get a shower and get dressed, and let's go to dinner."

"Great idea," Bill and Rob said at the exact same time.

"Okay, but it's going to take me a while. I look awful," Leah said.

Bill kissed her forehead. "Where are your towels? In the closet in the hall?" He got up from the bed and walked to the linen closet. He took out a big fluffy towel. "Here, we'll go downstairs and put some coffee on if that's okay. Take your time, Leah. And you look fine."

"You're more blind than I am, you son of a bitch. Blind as a fucking bat." Leah said, half laughing, half crying.

Bill laughed. "I love when you cuss."

She threw a pillow at him. She smiled.

"That's better, now get ready for dinner," Bill said as he caught the pillow in midair and left the room with Julie and Rob.

While Leah got ready to go to dinner, Julie put the news on the TV. She sat with Rob and Bill at the dining room table sipping coffee.

"And turn that damn news off!" Leah yelled from upstairs.

Julie had to laugh. "Even when she's this depressed, she has a sense of humor." Julie was watching Bill.

He took a deep breath and said, "Okay, yes, I told her. And you'll never believe what she said."

"What?" Julie asked.

"She told me to never stop loving my wife. She isn't jealous, upset, or anything. If anything, I think she'd be upset if I didn't still love her. She told me I should see my in-laws again. I swear, she is unbelievable."

Julie and Rob nodded in agreement. Rob said, "That doesn't surprise me at all. She gets it, Bill, she really does."

"Then why does she want to die? What if she did take her life? How could anyone not love her? I mean, she's so honest, so endearing, so real. I feel alive again because of her. She's everything to me. Everything. And she's so damn beautiful and wants to be with me of all people," Bill looked away.

Very softly, Julie said, "Leah isn't with anyone she doesn't want to be with, Bill. Believe me. She has very strong standards of who she associates with. She never compromises on that. She has some very serious issues is about all I can say, Bill. I'm sorry. One of them is her physical appearance, and the other is a real big fear of being abandoned. Just love her. Please just love her. Her self-esteem is practically nonexistent because of some of the things she's been through."

He looked at Julie and almost whispered. "I do love her. I love very much. I told her how I feel about her. I just don't know what's in her head. I want her to always know how much I love her. She told me about her parents. She never said so, but it isn't rocket science to know she's afraid of being abandoned. The look on her face said it all.

Thing is, I'll never abandon her. I love her, damn it, and I hope she believes me when I tell her I love her."

"She does, Bill. Trust me, and she loves you. It's all within herself. Just give her time, okay?" Julie said, and looked straight into Bill's eyes.

Rob and Julie smiled. They both took hold of Bill's hands. No words were needed. Bill knew it would be all right somehow. Bill trusted them completely. He smiled and nodded in agreement. His eyes sparkled a little.

"I do have one question," Bill said. "Maybe she should get some help?"

"Bill," Rob said, "she doesn't have and can't afford insurance. She couldn't pay for what she needs." Bill looked at him and Rob knew exactly what he was going to say. "Forget it, Bill. She's more stubborn than you are, and she's very proud. She never asks for help with anything. Everything she has she got for herself and by herself, and she will always be that way. And don't ever tell her I said anything, please."

At that point, Leah called to them from upstairs. "I'll be down in a minute, okay? Would one of you mind taking the dogs out, please?"

"I'll take them," Julie said.

"I'll go with you, hun," Rob said, and they headed for the backyard with the dogs.

Leah came down the steps and walked into the dining room where Bill was sitting. He looked up at her.

She had on a teal blue shirt and a nice pair of black slacks. Her hair fell gently on her shoulders, and her face was perfect. She smiled.

"You are beautiful, Leah," Bill said and stood up. He gave her a hug. Leah did look beautiful, although not even Bill could convince her. The depression would not leave. She knew, however, that she was very lucky to have friends like this.

When Julie and Rob brought the dogs in, Julie said, "Okay, I'm starving. What'll it be tonight?

Leah stood close to Bill. She put her arm around his back. "Would you guys mind if we got Chinese?"

Julie smiled and said, "I was hoping you'd say that."

The waiter came to take their order. "I'll go last," Leah said. "I haven't made up my mind yet."

Julie giggled. "Oh no, that means she's real hungry."

Bill looked at Julie, then at Rob and Leah, and said, "Uh-oh."

Rob laughed. "Uh-oh is right. You ain't seen nothin' yet. When she's this hungry, watch out."

The waiter came over to Leah. "Okay, I'll have a bowl of wonton soup, an egg roll, pork fried rice, honey-glazed shrimp, boneless pork ribs, a small order please."

Bill interrupted, "Thank goodness for that." Everyone laughed. Leah gave him a dirty look, which made him laugh even harder.

Leah continued, "Chicken and snow peas with white rice, and ice cream for dessert, with whipped cream." She took a sip of her wine and continued, "Oh, and extra fried noodles please."

Bill laughed and said, "And look at her, tiny as can be. I put on twenty pounds just listening to her order dinner."

Leah felt better, even though she knew it was a false and only temporary. The extra wine kept the calmness for her. She looked at Bill and he smiled at her. She thought to herself, *Oh God, I love him so much.*

When Bill took Leah home, he was very quiet. He couldn't find the words to say what he was feeling. He walked her to her door, and then inside. Leah put one light on.

"Leah," Bill said softly, "I love you." Then, he took her in his arms and kissed her with a passion that shocked Leah. He held her so close that she felt his heart beating. She, in turn, clung to him.

They looked at each other, and Leah let out a huge breath. "Wow, what was that all about?"

Bill smiled. "I'm just so damn glad you're still here. When I saw you earlier today, lying there, I thought—"

Leah interrupted, "I'm sorry. I really am. I'm just—"

He put his hand on her lips. He hugged her. "I love you, Leah. Whatever it is that is eating you alive, I wish you'd let me help you."

She couldn't answer him. She just put her arms around his neck and held him tight.

Bill knew he had to accept that as her answer, at least for now.

Leah had taken the next day off work just to get some rest. Bill didn't tell her, but he went to her job to talk to Macie. When he walked in, she was on the phone. She looked up right away and motioned that she'd only be a minute. She smiled, hung up, and said, "Hi. Nice to see you. What can I do for you?"

Bill smiled. "I wanted to thank you for covering for Leah these last few days. She's had a very rough time of it. And this is for you, Macie, for taking care of things here for her," Bill said and handed her a giant box of chocolates.

Macie smiled. "Godiva Chocolates! How nice of you. You didn't have to, but it just so happens these are my favorite!" She opened the box, took a piece, offered one to Bill. He politely shook his head no. Macie ate the piece of candy as if it were laced in gold. "Mmm, thank you so much. You now I love Leah. She's a great friend and a great boss. We know each other inside and out. I know she has issues. I don't know exactly what they all are, but I know she's troubled. I'd do anything for her. I have to tell you, since she met you, though, she's been happier than I've seen her in the years I've known her."

This made Bill smile. He said, "Thank you. She's a great girl. I do want to ask a favor of you. Can I give you my number? I mean, in case she calls out like this again?"

"Of course. I think that's a great idea. Better yet, let's exchange numbers just in case." Macie wrote her number down on a piece of paper. "Here you go. Don't hesitate to call me. She's a good girl, but sometimes she has trouble."

Bill nodded and wrote his number down also. "Thank you."

Macie smiled. "She's lucky to have someone like you who loves her so much."

Bill's face said it all. He was wondering how she could tell.

Macie was very, almost dangerously, outspoken, and she could tell what he was thinking. She giggled. "It's obvious, Bill. The way you look at her, the way you look when you talk about her." Macie shook her head. "Wow, she is one lucky girl. She's been a great friend to me. Thank you for being there for her. She's one of the strongest people I know, but she can and will break in a second."

Bill nodded. "Yes, I know. Thanks for your help. Keep in touch." He smiled and walked out of the office.

The next day, Macie came to work with coffee and donuts. Leah slipped money into her purse and said, "Thank you for covering for me. I was in a bad way."

Macie said, "I know, honey. I got you covered. And…too much money for one. And second, that man of yours. You'd better hang on to him."

Leah looked at her and sipped her coffee. She smiled and said, "I know."

"He is wild about you. That's all I can say." Macie laughed. "Don't blow it, kiddo,"

"I'm wild about him too. I don't understand this whole thing, but I think I choose not to even try and to just go with it. It was love at first sight, Macie. I looked at him, and that was that."

The next day, Bill called Leah in the evening. She was sitting on the couch watching TV when she answered the phone. "Hello."

"Leah, hi. How are you?" Bill sounded so concerned.

"I'm okay, thanks. I really am," Leah said. She was so glad to hear from him.

"I have something I want to talk to you about. Do you have a minute?" Bill asked.

"Sure, is something wrong?" Leah began to worry.

"Oh no. I've been thinking about what you said, you know, about visiting my in-laws and I think you're right. I should."

"I know they'll be glad to see you," Leah said.

"Will you come with me?" Bill asked.

Leah didn't quite expect that, but she said, "If you want me to, of course. Do you think that's a good idea?"

"I do. I really want them to meet you."

Leah took a deep breath and let it out. "Okay, I'll be glad to." She was afraid, but knew she had to go if that was what he wanted.

"I'll call and set up a date and time," Bill said. He sounded almost frightened.

"Bill, it's the right thing to do. I can feel it," Leah said.

As they headed for his in-laws, Bill was very quiet. Leah tried to be brave, but she was so nervous.

"I want my in-laws to meet you, Leah, because of the way I feel about you and how I feel about my wife. Her parents were very good to me. I wasn't an in-law to them. I was their son. I know I hurt them very badly by not keeping in touch. But I know they understand. Still, they didn't deserve the way I treated them." Bill took her hand. He could tell she was nervous to say the least. "It'll be all right. They'll love you. I promise."

"They won't think I'm trying to take her place? Will they? 'Cause I'm not. She was your wife, their daughter."

Bill said quietly as they pulled up in front of the house, "That's exactly why I'm doing this. You can't take her place. I don't want you to. You are who you are. I love that. They'll be glad for me, believe me. They should know you, Leah."

"Bill, I don't know if I can do this." Leah began to feel terrified.

Bill looked at her with those beautiful blue eyes and said in a deep, powerful, but gentle tone of voice, "It's okay. They are good people, and they'll understand." He kissed her gently on her lips. "You can wait here if you'd like. I'll go to the door."

Leah smiled. "Okay." When Bill walked away, she took a piece of candy and a bottle of water from her purse and swallowed the candy. She closed her eyes and said to herself, "Hurry, please."

When the door opened, there stood Bill's mother-in-law. She smiled and said, "Bill, we missed you so much." Her aged eyes filled with tears. "I'm so glad you came."

He smiled. He patted his stomach. "Hello, Sara. I guess I've put on a few pounds since I last saw you. I'm so sorry I didn't keep in touch. Is Ed here? I'd like to talk to you both."

"Come in," Sara said. She was in her eighties. She looked older than Bill had anticipated. It made him uneasy and sorry for losing touch. She hugged him. "It's so good to see you." Sara led Bill in. "Ed, Bill is here."

Ed appeared in the doorway of the living room. "Bill, hello."

Bill couldn't make eye contact with Ed. He knew how much Ed was hurting, how much he himself had hurt them both by losing touch for so long. "I'm sorry, Ed. Very sorry. I couldn't function after she died. I just couldn't. You both were always so good to me. You became my family. Please try to understand."

Ed broke out into a big smile "It's okay. We understand. Did Sara tell you we had been thinking about you? And then you called?"

"Yes, she did," Bill said.

"So who is that girl in your car?" Ed asked and looked toward the window.

"Uh, she's um—"

"Good for you," Sara said.

Bill hesitated and then laughed. "You always knew me inside and out, Sara."

"Of course. We are family you know," she said with a sweet, understanding tone in her voice.

"Can we sit down for a minute?" Bill asked.

Sara and Ed nodded. Bill and Ed sat on the couch. Before Sara sat down, she asked, "Do you still drink, Jack?"

Bill nodded. "Sure could use it right now. Thank you."

"Coming right up," Sara said.

Bill and Ed had a Jack. Sara had a glass of white wine.

"What's on your mind, Bill?" Sara said.

"Well, the lady in my car. She's, well, I met her at a party. Totally by accident. Her name is Leah. I wasn't even going to go to the party. And, uh, neither was she. She came late, the seating got all messed up, so she was seated at the same table I was. I looked at her, she looked at me, we began talking, and, well, I'm going to ask her to marry me, if she'll even have me, and I'd like you to meet her. She is a very special lady. I told her about my wife, and that I still love and always will love her and she's fine with it. She told me to never stop loving her. Leah is someone I never thought I'd find. She is so unique, so unselfish. I can't explain her. When I saw her that night, our eyes met and I knew—"

Sara laughed and cut him off midsentence, "Bill, you haven't changed. You acted the same way when you wanted to ask our permission for our daughter to marry you. You have our blessing, Bill."

Ed said, almost yelling and laughing at the same time, "Bring her in. We'd love to meet her."

Bill was so relieved. He nodded. He had a huge smile on his face as he got up and went to the car.

He opened the door and said, "Leah, they want to meet you," and he reached for her hand. She took it and walked with him to the door. She was petrified.

Bill knew it. He could feel her shaking. "Leah, it's okay, really. Relax."

When Leah came in the house, Sara looked at her. She looked deep into her soul. Ed took her hand, and he too looked deep into her soul. They all knew this was a good thing. They hugged her. "Welcome, sweetheart," Sara said to her. "Will you stay for dinner? Please?"

"Only if I can help," Leah said, feeling, strangely enough, suddenly very comfortable.

Sara took her hand. "I'd love the help. Come into the kitchen with me, and we'll make these guys a dinner they won't soon forget."

Leah looked at Bill and smiled. He winked at her. She knew things were good.

Sara began to take things out of her refrigerator to make dinner. Sara smiled and said, "I put a roast in the oven earlier hoping you'd stay for dinner. Bill always loved my roast beef. What ya say about that for dinner, with some mashed potatoes, fresh green beans, a salad, and some homemade rolls? I have some real nice red wine too. Bill loves his red wine."

Leah nodded and laughed. She liked Sara right away. "Sounds perfect to me."

Sara was glad. "I bought a cake too, for dessert. I hope you like chocolate cake."

Leah smiled. "Who doesn't?"

Sara looked at Leah. She smiled. "Leah, you are so lucky. You have a great guy you know."

Leah smiled. "I do know. He is so special. I don't take him for granted."

Sara just smiled. "He loves you very much. I can tell by the way he looks at you and the look on his face when he speaks of you."

Leah smiled. "Sara, I love him with my whole heart and soul. I never thought I could feel this way about someone. I love him so much that it almost hurts."

"He was so good to our daughter," Sara said as she opened the oven to check on the roast. "Knowing how you feel about him makes me so happy." Sara paused for a second, almost looking like she was trying to compose herself. Leah understood how hard this must be for her. "You can start the potatoes and then snap the beans, okay? They're on the counter," Sara said.

"Sure." Leah thought this visit would be so awkward, but it was just the opposite. She could hear Bill and Ed talking in the living room. Sometimes it sounded serious, then they'd laugh out loud. "Sara," Leah said, "I love Bill so very much, and I promise I'll be good to him always."

Sara looked at Leah and put her hand on her shoulder. "I know you will, dear. Thank you."

Dinner was delicious. Bill sat next to Leah, Sara with Ed. The conversation was easy. After everyone finished dinner, Sara said, "Okay, time for a drink than dessert." Bill had his whiskey, as did Ed. Sara and Leah had wine. They sat for a short time at the table before Sara said, "Who would like a piece of cake?"

All at once, Ed, Bill, and Leah said, "I would."

Sara looked happy, but with a lonely loss in her eye. "Good, because today—"

Very quietly, Bill said, "Is her birthday. I never forget her birthday."

Sara was happy to hear that. "She would have turned fifty-one," Sara said and smiled a faint smile.

Bill looked at the cake. "Her favorite."

Sara and Ed just smiled. Sara said, "How great is this day? It's nice to have you both here today. It's been one of the loneliest days of our lives, until now. Leah, please make a wish and blow out the candle."

Leah didn't realize how young Bill's wife was when she died. It broke her heart. "I don't have a wish because it just came true. I've seen how strong and how fierce love can be, and it makes me feel good and so lucky to be a part of this. I never thought this kind of love and family could exist in this world. Thank you for letting me be a part of it." A tear fell from her face, yet she smiled. She blew out the candle.

Leah called Julie that night and told her what a wonderful time she had. She felt good, and Julie could tell. "Leah, please try to hang on to this feeling, this experience. When things get hard, remember this day. Promise?"

"I promise. It really was a very nice day," Leah said. "Speaking of birthdays, when Bill's birthday comes around, would it be all right with you if I made dinner? I mean, for all of us? I know you said you were going to have a party, but I'd like to do it. I want to invite Sara and Ed. They made me feel like I was a part of the family. It was so nice."

"Of course. I know Bill would love that. And from what you just told me, you have become part of their family."

"I actually felt that today. What a great way to feel. Thanks. I'm going to call it a day. I have to go to work tomorrow, and I'm beat," Leah said. She finished her glass of wine, settled down on her couch, put the television on, and soon fell fast asleep.

The next day was extremely busy. The phone was ringing off the hook, and customers were coming at a steady pace, wanting to see and adopt animals. That was a good thing.

Some were surrendering their animals. No matter what the circumstances, that was always sad. At one point, later in the day, there were many customers asking to see dogs. It wasn't uncommon for front desk employees to walk customers to the kennels when a member of the dog department was in the kennel area showing dogs. A group had formed. Leah walked them back, and went through the area to see how many dog department employees were in the area to help the customers. Just as Leah walked toward the back of the area, one of the young men in the dog department came through with a dog that had been adopted and returned three times. He had trouble getting him into the kennel. The dog stiffened his body and refused to go in. Leah turned to him and asked, "What's going on with him? He was adopted and I thought it was finally going well."

The young man who was holding the dog said, and his eyes filled with tears, "Going to hell is more like it. The family said they can't handle him. So many dogs come in here from who knows what kind of hell. So here he is, back again. He is a special-needs dog, and I just don't get why it won't work out for him. We explained to the family what his issues are and what he needs from a family, goddamn it! And they promised to adhere to it so he would finally have a home for the rest of his life. Makes me sick!"

He finally got the dog in the kennel. Leah stood and looked at the dog's face. He stood still in the middle of the kennel, looked around, looked at Leah and the young man, looked at the ceiling and then down, and his eyes became blank. In her heart she felt him shut down. Her stomach turned.

The young man was crying at this point, and said, "Look at his face, he's totally shut down. He's given up."

Leah began to cry. She reached out to pet him, as she had done many times before when his ambassador had him out for walks and playtime. She never once hesitated to go up to him and pat his head and give him a hug. He was one to be treated with caution because of his past and special needs, but he liked Leah, and she adored him. This time, he was nonreactive. Not wagging his tale and "smiling" that famous bully-breed smile. Leah looked up, and the department manager had come in by then. She too was crying. "My God, if he could talk, he'd ask us to end it for him. Look at him. All of the life has gone out of him."

Leah's whole body ached for this dog. "Oh my God, I can't stand the look on his face." She looked at the dog. "I'm so sorry, sweetheart," Leah said. She opened the door to touch his face. He let her, but again, no reaction. He just stood there, still, staring at nothing. Leah kissed his forehead, closed the door, and walked away crying.

When Leah got back to the front, Macie noticed she had been crying. "Honey, what's wrong?"

Leah shook her head. "I have to go to my office. I can't be out here."

She closed her office door, sat at her desk, put her head in her hands on her desk, and cried and cried.

Leah didn't hear the knock on her door or the door open. "Hey…"

Leah looked up, and Bill was standing in the doorway.

She looked at him and smiled through her tears. "Macie called you, didn't she?"

"Let's just say I heard what happened. I'm sorry, so sorry," Bill said. "Can I come in?"

"Yeah," she whispered. "I hate this world most of the time. The look on that dog's face is exactly how I felt the day my mother left, and then my father discarded me. Only he can't speak for himself." Leah continued to cry for the dog.

He nodded. "I know. It's a rough place, more often than not." He took his hand from behind his back and handed her a small white box. "I had to run to the bakery for work, and I thought I'd bring you a little something."

She smiled while still crying, took the box, and opened it. Inside were two giant buttercream cupcakes. "You did not. You lie. You heard I was upset and came here. How come you're so damn nice?"

Bill just smiled. "Because I love you so damn much. I can't stand to see you hurting." He reached over and took a tissue from her desk and wiped the tears from her face. He pulled a chair next to her, put his arm around her, and sat for a minute.

"I must look like a train wreck. I'm sorry," Leah said as she dipped her finger in the icing of one of the cupcakes and licked her finger. "Mmmmm," she said.

Bill couldn't help but laugh. "You're the best-looking train wreck I've ever seen. Are you going to be all right? You're really worrying me."

Leah shook her head. "I'll be fine. This isn't the first time, and it won't be the last. We know these animals. Especially ones like this who have been here long and been through a hell we'll never know. It makes me sick, so damn sick. I often wonder if they had been one of the prettier or fancier breeds, would this have happened? People tend to coddle the beautiful ones, don't they? Just like with people. Damn it anyway."

Bill nodded in agreement. "Yes, they do." He took her hand and held it for a while.

Leah looked at Bill. "You are the sweetest thing in this world, besides these cupcakes. Want one?" She smiled.

"No, thanks. I have a confession to make. Already had two, and I want you to give one to Macie."

Leah smiled. "Okay, I will. I'm sorry you had to see me like this."

Bill smiled. "You know what—"

Leah interrupted, "Yes, I do. You are so special. Now get back to work. I'll be fine. Let's do something special or different for dinner tonight, okay?" Leah said as she ate the cupcake. "Wow, this is good." She had some of the icing on her lip. Bill reached over and wiped it off and smiled at her.

Bill kissed her forehead. "See you later. Seven?"

"Yes, and not a minute later, please," Leah said. "I have to get out of here as fast as I can today."

"You got it," Bill said and left.

Leah walked back to the front. She handed Macie the box with the cupcake in it. "Here, this is for you. From Bill."

Macie smiled. "Oh, thank you!"

Leah smiled at Macie. "You're welcome."

"Are you all right?" Macie asked Leah.

"Yes, I am. I just hate the way this world is. I hate it," Leah said and sat down by her computer.

Macie took a bite of the cupcake. "This is delicious! Be sure to thank Bill for me."

Just then, one of the volunteers walked in. She did a lot for the rescue on her days off and helped at the rescue in a number of ways after work. She came to the front desk. "Hi you guys," she said.

"Diane, how are you?" Macie asked.

"Good. I have the day off, so I thought I'd come help. Do you need me here or in the cat or dog department?"

"I don't know," Leah said. "Hang out up here for a while. It's good to see you." Leah liked Diane a lot. She made her laugh, and Leah appreciated her dedication to animals.

Macie looked at Diane and asked, "So what's new?"

"Well," she said, with a sarcastic sort of smile, "I met this guy today at the repair shop when I was getting a headlight put in my car. He was waiting on me and then asked me for my phone number. I'm not sure why. Didn't think he needed it to change the dumb light."

"Did you give it to him?" Macie asked.

"Well, yeah. I thought maybe he needed it for, well, I don't know. He was half my age and real good-looking." Diane smiled and laughed. "Maybe he's looking for a cougar," she said and looked at Leah, and they laughed.

Macie just looked at Diane.

"You do know what a cougar is, don't you?" Diane asked Macie.

"Yes. A car," Macie answered.

Diane looked at Leah, who in turn looked at Diane. Macie looked completely confused.

"She has no idea," Leah said.

They burst out laughing and Diane said, "Macie, a cougar is when a younger man goes for an older rich woman. She's the cougar."

Macie just stared at Diane. Leah couldn't stop laughing. "Oh my God, this is just what I needed," Leah said. "My stomach hurts from laughing! Oh my God! This is too funny!"

Macie laughed equally as hard. "I didn't know."

This made them all laugh even harder.

Bill's birthday finally came. Leah was excited to have Bill, Julie, and Rob over for dinner. She made sure she looked as good as she could. Still, she couldn't feel pretty. She fought the sadness and depression that seemed to be chasing her. Tonight was a special night. She couldn't give in to it.

Leah was in the kitchen when the doorbell rang. She called, "Just a minute," and reached into her purse. She took a piece of candy and then grabbed her glass of wine on the counter to wash it down. She went to the door.

Bill was first to arrive. She was so happy to see him. She smiled and opened the door. "Happy Birthday," she said and let him in.

He smiled. "Thank you." He had his hand behind his back. "I have something for you."

She laughed. "It's not my birthday, it's yours."

"I know, but I wanted to give you this." And he handed her a purple rose.

She took it and said, "I love it. Come on in. Let's not stand in the hall. Come and sit down for a minute." They walked into the living room. Both her dogs were glad to see Bill. Ricky was jumping all over him, and Honey limped over to greet him.

"Do you know what a purple rose stands for?" Bill asked.

She didn't answer him. Leah looked at him and walked out of the living room. A few seconds later, she came back and handed him a purple rose. "Yes," Leah said and smiled. "Love at first sight. I got this for you this morning. I hope you like it."

Bill looked at her. They both laughed.

"I'll put them in a vase on the table," Leah said.

Bill stood up and walked over to her and put his arms around her. "You and me. It feels so nice."

Leah couldn't believe how he loves her. She loves him. "I'm lucky to have you, Bill." She hugged him.

Bill laughed. "You can't even get your arms around me."

She looked at him. "That's because your heart is so big." She kissed him gently on his lips.

"You've made me very happy. You know that," Bill whispered. He took her arm and walked her into the kitchen. To get to the kitchen, they had to go through the dining room. Bill looked at the table. "Can I help with anything?"

"No, thanks. I'll make you a drink. Would you like some of that awful whiskey or some wine?" Leah asked and then sipped her wine.

Bill had to laugh. "I'm sorry, but to this day, every time I think of that night I have to laugh. I shouldn't have done that to you. I'll have some Jack if you have it. I'll have wine with dinner if that's all right."

Leah laughed. "It was funny, but not very nice." She poured him a glass of Jack Daniel's. "I hope you like the wine I bought to go with dinner."

"Dinner smells great. What did you make?" Bill asked.

Leah handed him his drink. He smiled and took a sip.

"Beef Burgundy stew. I hope everyone likes it," Leah said.

Bill laughed. "If it tastes half as good as it smells, everyone will love it."

"Bill, I have something to tell you. I think I should have said something, but honestly, until just now, I thought this would be a nice surprise for you." She took a deep breath and wished the candy and wine would kick in. "I asked Sara and Ed to join us for dinner tonight. I hope that's all right."

"I wondered why you had six places set. I think that's great, Leah. Thank you. I feel so much better being back in touch with them. They're so special to me. You don't realize what you've done for me by suggesting I see them again." Bill said with a huge smile on his face.

She just looked at him. She did that a lot, just taking him into her soul.

"What?" Bill asked, noticing how she was looking at him.

"Oh, nothing," she said and looked away smiling.

"Tell me," he said.

She looked back at him. "Well, I was just thinking, that if this were my last minute on earth, I would want you to be my very last memory."

He looked at her and smiled. It was a different smile. He knew how much she loved him. This made him feel very good.

She took another drink from her glass. She smiled at him.

Bill wanted to ask her then why she wants to die. Why is she so depressed. He worried about her. She was so fragile at times, and he knew it. He was close to asking, when the doorbell rang.

Leah walked to the living room and peeked through the window and said to Bill, "It's Ed and Sara. Come into the living room and sit down. I'll get the door, and you can talk while I finish up in the kitchen. Julie and Rob will be here soon."

Leah opened the door. "I'm so glad you came tonight."

Sara handed her a box of chocolates as she and Ed walked in. They noticed that Bill was already there.

Leah brought them into the living room. "Please, sit down and make yourselves at home." Ricky and Honey came over to greet them. Leah laughed. "These are my kids. I also have two very lazy cats who never do anything but sleep and eat. They're up in my bedroom sound asleep, waiting for room service." Leah opened the candy and put it on the coffee table. "Thank you," she said, "and Ricky, no chocolate for you two." He looked at her and had a disappointed look on his face. This made everyone laugh. Leah took the box and walked to Sara and Ed. They took a piece and Bill followed.

Leah took a piece, popped it in her mouth, and said, "I'm going to tend to dinner. Julie and Rob should be coming any second. Bill, will you let them in and do the introductions please?"

"Glad to," he said. He, Sara, and Ed talked while Leah went into the kitchen.

"Sara, Ed, what would you like to drink?" Leah called as she got glasses out of the cabinet.

"The usual," Ed answered."

"Coming up," Leah said. She grabbed her wineglass and refilled it. She brought Ed and Sara their drinks.

Just then, the doorbell rang. It was Julie and Rob. Bill started to stand up. "I got it, Bill. I'm right here," Leah said. She opened the door. "Hey, you two. Thanks for coming. C'mon in and sit down." Leah took them to the living room. "Sara, Ed, this is Julie and Rob."

Sara looked at them, and she and Ed just smiled. "Nice to meet you both," Sara said.

"Julie and Rob are our closest friends," Leah said to Sara and Ed. Then she turned to Julie and Rob. "Sara and Ed are Bill's in-laws."

Julie and Rob smiled at them. "It's a pleasure," they both said at the same time.

"I'll get you both a drink, check on dinner, then I can sit for a few minutes and visit." Leah went back to the kitchen and returned shortly with drinks for Julie and Rob.

Leah thought things might be uncomfortable, but she had begun to relax, and somehow she thought Sara sensed her concern. "Leah," she said, "you have a beautiful home. This is so nice of you to have us here and to celebrate Bill being old."

Leah just looked at her. Bill let out a huge laugh and said, "Thanks a lot."

"You're very welcome," Sara said and giggled. Her face lit up when she laughed. Ed just shook his head.

During dinner, the conversation flowed. All of Leah's concerns had disappeared. Everyone got along beautifully.

"Dinner is wonderful, Leah," Bill said.

"I agree," Ed said and took another bite.

"So," Bill said, and looked at Sara and Ed, "did you know that Leah has a horse?"

"No, we didn't. How nice," Sara said. "Did you grow up on a farm?"

Leah smiled and shook her head, "No. Don't I wish."

"Do you do any competitive riding?" Ed asked.

"No, he's a rescue. All my horses for the last I don't know how many years have been rescues and unrideable because of lameness or other issues. Harry, that's my horse's name, believe it or not, I think he is rideable. But I don't know if anyone has ever been on him, and I'm not going to be the first," Leah said and sipped her wine.

"Oh, how interesting. Did you ever ride?" Sara asked.

"Yes, years ago," Leah said, "even won a blue ribbon once."

"Wow!" Bill said. "You never mentioned that."

Julie laughed. "She's too modest. It was a wonderful ride. She and her horse, Socrates, were so great!"

"I remember," Rob said and smiled. "You were too funny, Leah. When they announced she had won, she jumped up and down and started screaming. She was out of control."

Bill looked at her. He had a gentle look in his eyes.

"What?" Leah asked. "I worked for months on that ride."

Bill chuckled. "I'm sure. It's just that's so true to form for you, to just be you, no matter where you are. Since the blue ribbon is out in the open, what did you win it for? I mean, how do they judge?"

Sara and Ed saw the look on Bill's face. They then looked at each other, and smiled.

Julie and Rob saw the interaction. Rob winked at Julie. She just smiled.

"Well, there's a number of things to be judged on, different categories or disciplines. I did dressage, which a person has to do certain things in a timely manner at letters that are placed along the riding ring. I loved doing musical dressage, and this one time I showed in a musical dressage class. I had to write the routine myself, choose music to match the horse's gate, include all gates, walk, trot, canter, circles, stopping, and keep it at five minutes. I started working on it in April. The show wasn't until October. Socrates and I practiced every day for hours. He loved it. When I played the tape, he got this look on his face, and riding him was so easy. It was always easy because he was the most easygoing horse, but he could be stubborn, and at times he'd make up his mind that he just was not going to do what I asked. If I asked him for the canter when he wasn't in the mood, he'd walk fast. Stinker!"

Everyone laughed, and Sara said, "Wow, that sounds hard to do, to write a routine like that I mean."

Leah smiled. "It was, but I loved every minute of it. Dressage is like a tranquilizer. You have to concentrate so hard, there's no room to worry or think about anything else. I miss those days."

"It was a fun time," Julie said.

After dinner, as things go, the men went into the living room to have a drink and talk. The women, in the kitchen to clean and get dessert ready.

As they cleaned and made fresh coffee, Sara went over to Leah and whispered, "So Julie and Rob are the couple Bill helped out all those years ago. He never said a word, but my daughter told me about them."

Leah was a little surprised, and caught off guard. She knew how Bill didn't want things like that talked about. Bill would be so upset if he knew it was even spoken of. "Sara, yes but you know how he is. I never told a soul."

"Well, honey, our daughter told us because she was so over-whelmed by his kindness. She loved him totally, and this sort of thing only reinforced her love for Bill. You have a gem on your hands, you know."

Leah nodded and smiled. "Believe me, I know. I don't know why it happened, but it did. The whole thing, our meeting, was a total accident."

Sara put her arm around Leah. "No, I don't think so. I'm so glad he found you, or you found him, however it happened. He is a unique one of a kind man. You, Leah, are perfect for him. Please take good care of him. He loves you. I can see it in his eyes. I know him inside and out, and you are his love. Our daughter is smiling down on both of you from heaven."

Leah wanted to cry, but she couldn't because of the joy Sara gave her. "Sara, I will love this man forever, I promise you."

Sara gave Leah a big hug. "I knew you were right for him the minute I met you."

Leah took her hand. "Sara, no one ever told me your daughter's name."

Sara looked away, then deep into Leah's eyes. "Her name is Sara. Ed insisted on naming her after me because I was told I couldn't have children." Sara looked away for a second then laughed. "No one tells me what I can and can't have!"

Leah really liked Sara. So did Julie. They both hugged her. "Sara, I need dessert," Leah said.

Sara laughed. "I know. Bill told me how you pack it away and stay thin as a rail."

Julie asked, "What is for dessert anyway?"

"I made homemade apple pie. I hope everyone likes it," Leah said.

Julie looked at Sara. "Oh my God, her homemade pies are so good! Everything is from scratch!"

Bill stayed at Leah's after everyone left. They were sitting on the sofa in the living room. "Today was great, Leah. Thank you."

Leah smiled. "I'm glad you had a nice time. Happy birthday." And she leaned over and kissed his lips.

Things were going very well for Bill and Leah. One wintry night, Bill and Leah were sitting on the couch at Bill's, watching a movie. There was a nice fire in the fireplace. Leah was leaning on Bill's side. He had his arm around her. The movie was ending and Leah was crying.

Bill rubbed her shoulder. "Are you all right?"

"Yes. This movie just hit a nerve, I guess. I had an out-of-body experience, many years ago, just like the girl in the movie. It was very emotional."

Bill looked at her. "You never told me about this." He could tell it was very difficult for her to talk about it.

She shrugged her shoulders and wiped her face. "Who wants to hear this kind of stuff anyway? Who even cares? I talk way too much. Even the night we met I rambled on about my horses—"

Bill interrupted. "That was one of the things I loved about you from the start. You were so willing to share yourself with me. I forgot about myself, I enjoyed your story about all your horses. I enjoyed you, I felt so alive for the first time in years."

Leah sat up and wiped her face. Leah smiled. "You make me feel good, Bill."

"What happened? It must have been very traumatic for you."

Leah laughed a little. "I don't think of it like that. It was actually a beautiful experience, but deeply emotional. It was a peaceful journey." Leah took a deep breath. "My health went to hell in a handbasket when I was twenty-nine. Long story short, I was so sick. I spent a month in the hospital, and then the day after I had to have surgery, I started to bleed out. They rushed me back to the OR. I heard what they all said about my blood count being dangerously low, and a few other things. All the while, hearing all the commotion, I'm feeling very calm and I'm going through, in my head, everyone I know who would be all right without me. I came to the conclusion that everyone would be. I even felt the presence of an uncle of mine that I was very close to and my dog that I had during my teens, the one I told you about when I stood there at my father's new place, thinking we were welcome. I knew they were there, waiting for me. I couldn't wait to see them again. Then,"—she paused—"then I thought about my dog I had at the time. She was so damaged, so needy. She stuck to me like glue. I knew I couldn't leave her. That's when I decided I had to come back. At that point, it was like someone grabbed me by the scruff of my neck and pulled me back to earth." Leah laughed and rolled her eyes. "All of this because the doctors wouldn't believe I was as sick as I was trying to tell them, and the insurance company wouldn't pay for the things I needed, which is the reason, I'm sure, the doctors wouldn't do anything. I know it sounds silly, but I still think of that dog's face and how she'd be so alone if I didn't come back. I'm not even sure why she loved me so much. Friends of mine were babysitting her, and they told me she was a mess. Every time someone came to the door, or came in, she'd be looking for me. How pathetic. How sad for her. So I had no choice, really. I couldn't leave her." Leah stopped for a second, then said, "The look on her face when I finally did come home. I can't even describe it. Her eyes did this funny thing, like they were smiling. I held her forever that after-noon. But anyway, it was so peaceful knowing I was dying. It wasn't scary. Given the condition I'm in now, thanks to them well, just say if I could have gone, I would have. Oh, and here's something else that amused me. I told the doctor what my blood count was as they were whisking me away to the operating room. He asked me who told me and when I said I heard everyone talking, well, the look on his face was something I'll never forget. I think he thought I was nuts." She laughed. "It was pretty funny if you ask me."

Bill took Leah's hand and smiled. Bill decided not to ask her about the surgery. He somehow knew it was too much for her. He slightly laughed. He kissed her gently on her lips and said to her, "I'm glad you're here. I'm very glad you decided to come back." Bill paused for a second and then said, "I have a question for you."

"Sure, what? Will I ever stop talking?" Leah laughed.

"Uh, no, Leah. Not quite." Bill sat up straight and Leah looked at him.

"What then?" She was smiling, not realizing how serious he was being until she saw the expression on his face. "What's wrong?"

Bill shook his head. "Nothing is wrong."

"Okay, what then?" Leah said.

Bill looked at her with those beautiful blue eyes that Leah loved so much. He cleared his throat and said, "Will you do me the honor of becoming my wife?"

Leah just stared at him. She couldn't believe what she just heard. Her heart raced, and her head began to spin. "What?" She whispered.

Bill gently pushed Leah's hair off her shoulder. "I said, will you do me the honor of becoming my wife?"

At first, Leah couldn't seem to speak. After a few seconds, she said, "Yes, I will." Leah couldn't grasp this moment. Bill smiled. He reached in his pocket and handed her a small box.

"Open it, Leah," he said.

She looked at Bill, and she opened it. Inside was a beautiful diamond ring mounted in white gold. She just stared at it. "It's beautiful!"

"Try it on," Bill said, and took it from the box and put it on her finger.

"It fits!" Leah said, sounding like a child in a candy store. "How did you manage that?" She was so overwhelmed with emotions. She felt so good inside, but lurking in the depth of her heart now was a fear she couldn't seem to let go of, the fear of her on her wedding night.

Bill laughed. "I told my jeweler how petite you are. He guessed you take a size four."

Leah just looked at him. She leaned toward Bill and held him tight.

# CHAPTER 3

## *Desperate*

Later that night, Leah was on the couch watching TV. Leah kept going over what happened today. Leah could feel the panic and depression begin to set in. She felt there was no way for her to get away from it. It chased her down. She was getting deeper and deeper into this relationship, and now there was no way out that would spare Bill's feelings, or hers. It wasn't fair to Bill. She had a glass of wine, took a piece of candy, and called Julie. She began to cry.

"Hi, Leah," Julie said. "What'd you need?"

"Oh my God, Julie, I don't know what to do," Leah said, crying.

"What happened?" Julie asked.

"Well, I was at Bill's tonight. We had a perfect evening. We're watching this movie, we talked, and then do you know what he said to me?" Leah said and took a big gulp of wine.

Julie panicked. "No, what did he say? Is everything all right?"

In a loud voice, Leah said, "Is everything all right? Are you kidding me? He said to me, 'Will you do me the honor of becoming my wife?' I was so happy. So happy..."

Julie screamed, interrupting Leah. Rob heard her. "What's wrong?" he yelled.

"Nothing! Bill asked Leah to marry him! Oh my God!" Julie was so happy.

"Julie," Leah said, "did you hear me? He said, will I do him the honor of becoming his wife?" Leah was in a full-blown panic at this point.

Julie realized that Leah was very upset, and she began to worry.

"I keep saying this, but where the hell did this man come from? He is so everything a woman could want. I can't marry him. I said yes, I want to, but I can't marry him. It just came out when I said yes, but I can't." Leah couldn't control herself at this point. "Oh my God, Julie, what am I going to do?"

"Leah," Julie said, "calm down. Calm down and take a deep breath. Give the man a chance, okay? He loves you so much."

"Yeah, but he won't. He won't." Leah cried and cried.

"Leah, I want you to stay on the phone with me. Fix the couch, get comfortable, lie down, put on a rerun or the news…"

Leah interrupted, "You and that fucking news."

"Seriously, do what I say. You will marry him. You can't let go of this man," Julie said. Julie wouldn't let Leah talk about it. Abruptly, she said, "I'll call you in the morning. Stay with me on the phone until you fall asleep."

"I feel sick, Julie. I'm going to have some more wine and a—"

"Leah, how much have you had already?" Julie asked. "Do I have to come over?"

Leah didn't answer at first. "No, I want to be alone."

"Leah, do not do this to Bill again. You can't do this, and it's very inconsiderate of you to treat him like this," Julie said, begging her.

Leah felt so bad, she could barely stand it. "I can't do this, Julie. I just can't."

"I'm going to call Bill and have him come over. Maybe if you see him, you can get a grip on how much you mean to him."

"No, don't. He can't see me like this right after he asked me to marry him, are you crazy? I don't want to hurt him. I love him. That's exactly why I can't marry him. Oh God, what am I doing?" Leah was spinning out of control. "Julie, help me. I can't do this. I'm so frightened. I'm so horrible. I can't go on like this. I can't do this. I love him so much. I can't do this." Leah was sobbing. "I can't lose him but I know what will happen. Oh God I so feel sick. I just want to die."

"All right, I'm coming over," Julie said. She was so upset she yelled at Leah, "Do not do anything you'll regret! I'll be there soon."

Julie let herself in when she got to Leah's. Leah was on the couch. She had a glass of wine; it was almost empty. Ricky was lying beside her. He never took his eyes off Leah. Honey was lying on the floor by Ricky, looking up at Leah.

Leah looked at Julie. She began to scream at Julie, "What do I tell Bill on our wedding night? You tell me what I'm supposed to say to him, goddamn it! Goddamn everything! Goddamn me! Goddamn me!" She took a deep breath, "He already did! I can't fucking believe any of this. Fuck everything. What do you suggest I wear to bed? Huh? What? I'm not doing this anymore. I can't fight this depression. It's too quick to catch me and too strong for me to fight when I can't win anyway." Leah was out of control. She couldn't calm down.

"I'm sorry this happened to you, but I can't help you. I think he will love you regardless. I know he will. I know Bill. He is a beautiful man who needs you. Do you realize how hurt he is? How a recluse he was? He trusted himself to you. He opened himself up to you, Leah. I know Bill inside and out, and what happened to him damn near killed him. I know it killed his spirit. Now he's letting himself be involved with you. This isn't easy for him. He's given himself to you because he loves you so much, and you're just going to throw it in his face?"

Leah looked at her. She didn't know what to say. She just sat and drank what was left in her glass. "I'm sorry. I love that man more than I can tell you. I just can't do this to him. He deserves more than a woman like me. He deserves a beautiful, normal wife. Oh my God, I feel so bad I can't stand it."

Julie sat by Leah and held her. "Let me call Bill. He'll come over. We can have coffee. I'll call Rob too. We can play cards, watch a movie, or even better, a crime-show rerun. You love that crazy stuff."

Leah tried to pull herself together. "No, he can't see me like this. Would you just stay with me until I fall asleep? I'm really afraid of how I'm feeling right now. I don't feel very good at all."

Julie pushed the hair out of Leah's eyes. "Oh, I'm not leaving you alone tonight, kiddo. I'm staying here. I'll take your dogs out, and make you some tea. Close your eyes and think about Bill. Think about those blue eyes you are always talking about. Think about how much he loves you."

Leah did manage to smile. "He does have the most beautiful blue eyes I have ever seen. That's what got me the night we met. Oh, God, those eyes." Leah was asleep soon, even before her tea was ready.

Julie called Rob. "Rob, I have to spend the night. She's in one of her depressions. It's bad and I can't leave her. She's the worst I've ever seen her."

"I understand. No problem. Take care of her. I wish she would tell Bill, but I guess she won't. Let me know how she is. If Bill happens to call, what should I say? I have a feeling he'll call to tell us she accepted his proposal."

"I agree and I don't know. You'll think of something. He doesn't need this tonight. Maybe tomorrow will shed a different light on things for Leah. God she scares the hell out of me."

Leah woke up in the middle of the night. Julie was fast asleep on the love seat across the room. Leah went into the kitchen and poured herself a glass of wine. Then she went to her room, opened her dresser drawer, and took out a bottle of pills. Her candy. She put the television on, went through the channels, and stopped at an old crime show. She cried. She counted the pills. "Just enough," she said to herself, "to finish this hell." Leah slowly poured the pills into her hand. She stared at them and drank her wine. She thought about Bill. Then, she thought about Bill on their wedding night. "I can't do this," she said. "I'm finished," she raised her hand to her mouth.

"What the hell are you doing?!" Julie yelled from the doorway. "Damn you!" She ran over to Leah and hit her hand knocking the pills to the floor.

Leah just stared at her. She yelled, "You fucker! How dare you!"

Julie was so angry. "What the hell is wrong with you anyway? I thought we worked this out. Are you really going to put the man you love through this again? After all this?"

"Fuck you, Julie. I'm sitting here watching TV. All these beautiful women in bathing suits, sexy beach outfits, tight dresses, the men are after them. Look at you. You are one of them. You think any man would want me? Really? I'm fucking done. I don't want to be here. I am finished!" Then Leah screamed, "How the hell dare you try to stop me!"

"How the hell dare I stop you?" Julie screamed. "Because we love you, you fucking bitch! Because Bill loves you, we love Bill, and I know you love him too!" Julie rubbed her forehead. "I have such a headache from worrying about you and trying to talk sense into you. Bill loves you. He asked you to marry him for heaven's sakes. I'm sorry, Leah, but something is wrong here and something has to give. How many pills did you have? We have to get them off the floor so your animals don't get them."

Leah didn't answer.

Julie had picked up a handful. She watched Leah and thought she saw more in her hand. She went over to Leah and took them from her. "How many more?"

Leah looked at her. "I don't know. I counted thirty to be sure I'd go out quick."

"We have to find them. You need some help, and I mean some serious help, goddamn it. Let me call someone." Julie said.

"I need to be normal again, to feel like a woman, to look at myself and not want to throw up. That's the only help I need, and you can't give that to me or force me to do anything. If you bring me to a hospital, I'll leave. Being in a hospital is what almost killed me in the first place and is why I ended up like this." Leah took a deep breath. "Can we please not do this? I feel awful."

Julie sat on the bed. "Let's just get the rest of the pills off the floor. You have to promise me you won't try this again, Leah. I mean it."

Leah just looked at her. "I can't promise. I'm sorry. I won't promise," she said and reached for her glass of wine. "Julie, when I get this depressed, it feels as if the bottom falls right out from under me, like a trap door opens suddenly and I fall. Then I actually feel like the air itself is drowning me. I feel like I'm in a huge hole in the ground, and I'm looking up trying to get out, but I can't climb out.

I'm totally smothered by it." Leah took a deep breath, ran her hand through her hair, and said, "Believe me, Julie, I want to be happy, but I can't do it. Not being like this."

Julie began to cry. "I know, Leah, I know. We love you. You can't go on like this."

Leah found the rest of the pills and put all of them away in the bottle and held it tight. She sat back down on the bed next to Julie and finished her wine. "I'm so depressed. I'm so exhausted. So exhausted from living like this." Leah put her face in her hands. "I don't want to live anymore. I just don't."

"Not good enough. I'm going to go to Bill about this. This is very serious," Julie said in a very soft tone.

"No, please don't, Julie. Please," Leah said. "I'll tell him tomorrow. I will."

Julie didn't answer her. She just put her arm around Leah. "Oh God," Julie said out loud. "You'll tell him what? Why you're so depressed or that you were going to try to take your own life? Which, both? You are not being fair to him."

"Well, fuck all of you. I tried to get help. I had to almost die before anyone would believe how sick I was. That was too late and too bad for me, I guess. No one wants to talk about people like me. Just sweep me under the rug, and I'll go away. I'm going to tell Bill that I have these bouts with depression, which he already knows, and that I had a bad one tonight. I can't marry him, I just can't." Leah took a deep breath. "But I want to so badly. God, I love him. I love him so much that I don't want him to be stuck with a freak like me."

Julie took Leah's hand. "Come on downstairs with me. Let's watch TV together, and no, not the news. I'm not going to let you kill yourself even in it kills me."

They both realized how silly that sounded, and they laughed.

"See, it feels good to laugh," Julie said as they went downstairs. "You know what I mean. What would we do without you? You, me, Rob, and Bill are a family. All we have is each other, and we need each other very much."

Leah didn't answer. She just smiled a faint little smile as they sat together and looked for something to watch on TV.

Leah whispered, "I'm dead in the water, Julie. I don't have the strength to keep going."

Sara and Ed were still up watching television when their phone rang. Sara walked to the phone. "Hello?"

"Sara, hello? It's me, Bill. I figured you and Ed were still up since you're such night owls."

Sara laughed. "We are. Is everything all right?"

"Yes," Bill said. His voice sounded very happy. "I, uh, called to tell you that I asked Leah to marry me earlier this evening, and she accepted!"

"Oh, Bill, that's great! Hold on," Sara turned to Ed. "Bill proposed to Leah, and she said yes!"

Ed smiled. "Tell him that's wonderful!"

"Ed is very happy for you. You're a very lucky man, you know. Leah is a great woman. A very special woman."

Bill got very quiet. He took a deep breath. "Yes, I know. Listen, we'd love it if you and Ed will come to our wedding. Of course, we haven't made any plans yet, but—"

Sara jumped right in. "You couldn't keep us away! Let us know if we can help with anything." Sara paused for a moment. "Bill, we are so happy that you're back in our lives. We missed you so much. You've always been like a son to us."

"I feel the same. You know how much I love both of you. We'll talk, okay?" Bill said.

"Yes, soon," Sara said. "Good night, Bill." She hung the phone up. She looked at Ed. He motioned for her to come sit by him on the couch. He put his arm around her, and Sara put her head on his shoulder. He patted her shoulder.

Sara looked up at Ed and said, "Thank you."

Ed gently kissed her lips.

Bill called Rob. "Rob, I have something to tell you."

Playing it cool, Rob said, "Okay, I think I know."

Bill smiled. "Oh, did Leah tell Julie?"

"Yes," Rob said, trying so hard to sound normal.

"Is Julie there?" Bill asked.

"No, I mean, yes, but she can't come to the phone. Bill, this is so great!"

"Rob, I'm so happy. I never thought I'd feel like this again. Will you be my best man?"

"Of course," Rob said. "I wouldn't have it any other way."

Bill chuckled. "Thank you, Rob. This is something I never thought would happen."

"Well, it did and you deserve this happiness. She's a good woman."

Bill said in a very soft tone, "Yes, she is."

"I'll see her tomorrow," Bill said. "I called Sara and Ed. They were very happy. I invited them to the wedding, and they accepted. I'm so glad they did."

"Bill, that's terrific!" Rob said.

"They were my family for so long. I was their son, not just an in-law. I think they're truly glad for me. It feels so good," Bill said.

Julie woke up early the next day. "Oh my God," she said out loud. "What a night." She fell asleep on the love seat, and had convinced Leah to stay on the couch. Ricky was crunched up at Leah's feet, Honey was asleep on the floor in her bed. Julie stumbled to the kitchen to make coffee. It wasn't even light yet. Julie came back into the living room and put the news on. She kept it low so Leah wouldn't wake up. She took the dogs out and, when she got back in, sat quietly on the love seat and drank a cup of coffee.

About half an hour later, Leah woke up. She rubbed her face and looked at Julie. "Julie, I'm so sorry about last night"

"You did it again, scared the living hell out of me and Rob. Leah, you have to get a grip." Julie got up, went into the kitchen, and got a cup of coffee for Leah. "Here. Drink this. I'll make something to eat."

Leah looked at Julie. "I have to use the bathroom. No telling how long I'll be, so wait till I get out before making something." She rubbed her face. "I don't feel well at all. I'm so damn depressed, Julie. I'm so sorry. Thank you for staying with me. It comes over me, and I can't escape from it, Julie. It's horrible. It's like a monster that holds me, with giant claws, and I can't move. Julie, when Bill asked me to marry him, it threw me into a tailspin of total panic. I was so happy, it was so beautiful. But when I said yes, and what else could I say, I realized," Leah stopped. She held her head and said, "I'm so in love with this man, it isn't funny. It's just when I got home, I began to feel it coming on, the depression and panic that now I'd have to stop the charade that I am normal."

"Leah, I know, I really do. Do you honestly think I wasn't depressed when I had cancer, and we were losing everything? I thought about dying so many times back then. I don't know what your life is like, but I do know depression. We are your friends, and we love you. Bill loves you. The difference between you and Bill is that he accepts himself. You don't, and it's killing you."

"It's not even near the same thing, goddamn it! And you know it!" Leal yelled.

"I know, but you can't hurt Bill like this, and you have to give him some credit. He's not some ass, you know. Leah, I truly believe that if you did anything to yourself, it'd be the end of him. He wouldn't be able to handle it." Julie walked into the kitchen. "Yell when you're ready for breakfast. I have to get home and get cleaned up for work after we eat. Then I'll be back to run you into work."

Leah knew Julie was right. She also knew that she couldn't fight the depression when it captured her. It was so much stronger than she was. It exhausted her completely. She has no control over it. All those years of burying her feelings, accepting no man would have her, and acting like everything was fine totally drained her.

While Leah was getting ready for work, her phone rang. "Hello…"

"Leah," Bill said.

"Hi, Bill. Good morning," Leah said. She was so glad to hear his voice.

"Just calling to say I love you, good morning, and I miss you. Can I pick you up from work tonight?"

She smiled. "Yes, of course." Without revealing the reason, she said, "I'm sure Julie would love a break." Leah took a deep breath and said, "Bill, I can't wait to see you. I really can't wait."

Bill smiled. "Same here. I called Sara and Ed to tell them you said you'd marry me. Leah, I asked them to the wedding."

"You beat me to it. Good." Leah was glad. "Bill, the way you asked me to marry you, well, I have to tell you, that was the most beautiful proposal. I want you to know I love you. No matter what," Leah said, fighting back tears.

"Are you all right?" Bill asked.

"Yes, I'm fine. I was just up late last night. I just want you to know I'll never stop loving you."

"I feel the same." Bill paused for a second, and he asked, "Are you going into work today?"

"Yes, have to. There's so much going on. Plus, I have to show off this ring and tell everyone we're getting married. I'm going to ask my friends from work to the wedding too."

He laughed. "You'd better! They've been good friends to you."

"Yes, I know." Leah smiled. "I'll see you tonight."

"See you later," Bill said and hung up.

Julie pulled up and honked the horn. "Gotta run, kids," Leah said to her dogs. She felt good and wished the feeling would stay. She decided she would try to remember what Julie told her.

When Leah walked into the office, she took a deep breath and decided to make it a positive day. After all, she had the man of every women's dreams who wanted to marry her. Macie was already there. Leah asked, "What are you doing here so early?"

"Oh, Trish called me. She had to leave for one of her kids. She said she called you, but you didn't answer and she had to run as soon as possible. Her kid has the flu or something."

Leah crunched her face. "Yuck. Thanks for covering. I must not have heard my phone, and I never thought to check it. I've been distracted. Would you like to know why?"

Macie smiled. "Yes, of course."

Leah put her left hand out.

Macie took her hand and screamed. "Oh my God!"

Everyone came running to the front office. Kallie looked very worried. "Is everything all right?!"

One of the guys asked, "Who do I have to beat up?"

Then Leah and Macie realized. "Oh, I'm so sorry," Macie said as she pulled Leah's hand out so everyone could see the ring and said, "Look at this!"

Everyone screamed and clapped. "Wow! What a rock!" Kallie said. "You two are adorable together!" She hugged Leah. "Congratulations!"

Leah couldn't stop smiling. "He's the best man on earth." In the back of Leah's mind was last night's bout with crippling depression. She knew she had the man every woman would want. Still, she couldn't escape the feelings of anxiety and depression when it takes over her.

Later that day, Julie called Leah at work. Leah picked up her phone and walked away from the desk. "Hello?"

"It's Julie. Just checking on you. Are you all right now?"

"Yes, Julie, thanks. Everyone here at work is so happy for us. They don't know all the details, but we all talk and we all have our own private hell, so when things go well, we're all so glad for each other. It's like a family here. And, Julie, speaking of family, I don't know what I'd do without you and Rob. I do have to go, though. Macie is out there by herself, and you know it can be a rough crowd sometimes."

"Yeah, and like you can beat up the bad guy."

Leah laughed. "I can."

Julie laughed very hard. "You watch too many crime shows from the seventies and eighties."

"Julie, I'm going to talk to Bill tonight. I have to let him know what happened,"

Julie was so relieved. "Yes, you do. If you need me, call. It'll all be all right."

Leah just smiled. "See you later." She hung up and went back to the front desk.

Finally, seven o'clock rolled around. Bill came into the rescue. Macie was at the front desk. "Hello, Macie. Is Leah ready?" he asked.

"Oh, yes. She's fixing her face for you, Bill," she said with a smile.

He laughed. "There's nothing to fix." He shook his head, and as he did, Leah walked up front.

"I'm ready to go," Leah said. Bill took her hand, and they walked to the car. He opened the door for Leah to get in.

Before Bill got in the car, and before he could see, she took the water bottle out of her purse and swallowed a piece of candy. As he got in the car, Leah turned to him and said, "I have something I have to tell you."

"Oh…what?" Bill replied.

Leah hesitated. "Well, I had a very bad night last night after I got home. I was very depressed. Julie came over, spent the night. When she fell asleep, I went to my room, and I…" She stopped.

"What?" Bill asked.

"I was going to end it. Julie walked in on me, and stopped me." Leah looked away from Bill. "Oh God, I'm so sorry."

Bill couldn't believe what she was saying. She could see it in Bill's eyes, how hurt and sad he was. Bill just looked at her. He knew she was deeply troubled and knew it had nothing to do with her love for him. He loved her. He took her hand. He kissed her lips, and looked her in the eye. "Leah, you were so happy last night."

Leah looked into his eyes. "I know. And crazy as it sounds, I still am. Bill, I'm sorry, I can't tell you how strong the depression is. It attacks me, hits me from behind. It's so fierce and overpowering that I can't get out of its way. It literally suffocates me. It feels like I can't breathe. It totally takes over."

Bill just held her. "What's so wrong, Leah?

"I can't—"

Bill interrupted her. He could tell she was pretty shaken up about telling him. "Okay, you don't have to. When you're ready, you'll tell me what this is all about. I love you unconditionally. I don't know how many times I have to say it before you believe me."

Leah knew he had more to say. She wasn't sure what to expect. She looked away from him. "I do know you love me, and you do know this has nothing to do with the way I feel about you."

Bill smiled at her and said, "Look at me." He took her chin in his hand very gently. He made her look at him. Those blue eyes pierced her soul. Then he said so quietly, "Yes, I do. I also have something that I have to tell you."

Leah saw the look on his face. She knew it was going to be serious. She began to worry if he was going to call the wedding off, and at the same time she almost hoped he would, preventing the inevitable ending of their relationship.

Bill read her face. He smiled at her and said quietly, "No, I'm not going to call off the wedding. I can't wait to have you as my wife, Leah." He smiled. Then he got serious again. "Years ago, I bought a gun. I was going to use it on myself. I didn't only lose my wife. We found out she was pregnant shortly before we found out her cancer returned. She went into premature labor. Our little baby girl was so tiny and fragile. We had a chance to hold her. Then, our little girl, she just died. She died in my wife's arms." Bill had a look on his face that had no words to explain how painful this was. Leah just looked at him. "I never witnessed a heart so broken until that day when I saw Sara's face. If a broken heart has a face, hers was that face. I'll never forget the look in Sara's eyes. Then she asked me if we can name her Angeletta." Bill looked down for a few minutes.

Leah held his hand and whispered, "Little Angel."

Bill smiled a sad smile, nodded, and he quietly continued, "I said yes, of course, because that is what she was." Bill paused again and said quietly, "Julie never told you any of this?"

Leah quietly said, "No, she didn't. She respects your privacy, Bill. She told me way back when you and I first met that there are certain things in your life that you will tell me if you want me to know. This is very painful for you, and I wish I could change it for you."

He took a deep breath and continued in a very quiet voice, "The night when I decided to end it, something came over me, and I changed my mind. I felt, strangely enough, calm. It was something I can't explain. Something told me not to go through with it. I was so sad, so distraught, devastated. I was sick over all that had happened. I was so depressed. I had cut myself off from everyone. I never knew that kind of loneliness, that kind of emptiness, that sense of loss. It was awful. Everything was spinning out of control, and I couldn't stop it. I let myself go. Just look at me." Bill looked at himself. He looked so sad. "I felt that I couldn't take another breath, but I changed my mind at the last minute." He paused for a minute, and then said, "Maybe it's because you were coming into my life. I don't know, but all I know is that if I had taken my life, I'd have missed out on you. You love me, and I'm not sure why you accept me as I am, but you do. Remember when I told you that your horse, Socrates, probably guided you into King's stall? He wanted you to be happy because he loved you so much. He knew how much you loved him and what you have to offer the animals. I can't help but think it was Sara who made me change my mind that night. She knew of you somehow. She always said, before she died, she wanted me to be happy, to find someone who will love me and I will love. She said she didn't want me to be alone." Bill took a deep breath and put his arm around Leah. "Well, I am happy again and not alone. Please, Leah, when you feel like you just can't take it any longer, just come to me. There's a lot of good to be had here on earth, and to me, you're every-thing. I love you. You know I do."

She nodded her head yes. She smiled. "You accept me for crying out loud! I'm the craziest bitch you'll ever find, but you love me any-way. And"—Leah took a long pause—"what about you? Your broken heart?"

Bill looked past Leah for a second. Then he looked back at her. "Oh, it was broken, believe me. It's an emptiness so deep that I'll carry it with me forever, but I think it's different, more severe for a woman. Sara carried our baby in her body…"

At that moment she realized this was the sadness she sensed the day they met. She looked him straight in the eye, closed her eyes for a moment, shook her head no, and said, before he could continue, "You loved Sara, and you carried her in your heart since the day you fell in love with her. Then, when she was going to have your baby, you carried them both in your heart. There is no difference. It all was just as heartbreaking for you, Bill."

Bill just looked at her. There was no need for him to say any-thing. He smiled at her, and she then knew another part of him, a sweet, caring, genuine, and so loving part of him. Even though none of this about him surprised her, this made her love him even more. And he knew another part of her, a part he would cherish forever.

After a few seconds, she asked, "Do you still have that gun?"

Bill held her close. "No, I don't."

Leah felt relieved. She sighed and said, "Good because I want you to be with me, always. I really do need you."

He smiled at her and said, "Exactly how I feel about you." He kissed her lips and held her. "We'll work it out, whatever it is that's troubling you. I promise. Leah, I can't lose you."

This made Leah feel something she couldn't put into words. She just knew he somehow felt he could get through that pain from long ago when he told her. This night, their bond grew even stronger.

She knew she couldn't lose him. How would it turn out? She knew she had a very special man in her life. She was so overwhelmed with emotions. Still, she was afraid of how it will end.

He took her left hand and kissed it.

"I love you," she said. "God, I love you, Bill."

Bill broke into that smile that she loved. His eyes were bright. "All right, then. I'm going to take you to the best restaurant in town and—"

Leah interrupted, "Your place, right?"

"Yes, my place. We're going to sit and talk, choose our wedding day, plan our wedding, hold hands, drink wine, laugh. And when I take you home, I'm going to walk you inside, kiss you on your lips, and we are going to live happily ever after."

Bill was so sincere. She wished he could understand. She looked at the ring on her finger. She looked up at Bill.

He just smiled. "Let's get going. We'll have a nice evening."

Meanwhile, in the office, Kallie caught sight of Leah and Bill sitting in the car. Unaware of their conversation, but seeing them together, she smiled and ran to get everyone together. She was a practical joker most of the time. She grabbed a big piece of paper and scribbled something on it. "Come on, guys, let's go to the window." They followed.

Just then, Leah happened to look over at the window. "Oh no…" she said and put her face in her hands.

"What?" Bill asked. Leah couldn't look up. She pointed to the window of the building. There, in the window, stood Kallie, Macie, and a few of the kids. They held a sign that had a huge heart with an arrow through it, a bunch of X's and O's, and on the bottom it said, "Love Birds!" All the kids and Macie were laughing. This of course made Bill and Leah laugh very hard. Bill could barely talk. "See what I mean? See what you'd miss? I think you have a very big fan club here."

Leah finally caught her breath. "Obviously they didn't know we were having a serious conversation. Oh brother, I know they'll tease the hell out of me tomorrow."

"And you deserve it after what you put all of us through," Bill said. He messed her hair and drove out of the parking lot.

She knew how lucky she was to have the people in her life that she did. Leah reached over and held Bill's hand as he drove.

At the restaurant, soft music was playing. Leah and Bill were talking while they waited for dinner to arrive. They nibbled on appetizers and sipped their drinks. "So what do you think of a September wedding?" Bill asked Leah.

"I think it'll be perfect, Bill. Can we have it early in September, so the weather will still be nice?"

"That's perfect," Bill said. "I was thinking, would you like to have an outdoor wedding? I could ask Julie and Rob if we could have the wedding in their yard, you know, I thought it'd be kind of romantic since we met there."

Leah had the biggest smile on her face. "I can't believe you. What a perfect idea!" Leah sipped her wine. "Maybe an evening wedding? Around six? What do you think?"

"I think that's exactly how it should be, Leah." Bill smiled at her.

"I'll do my best to be the most beautiful bride. I want to make you so proud of me," Leah said.

"Too late, already have," Bill said and winked at her. "You'll look beautiful!"

Leah rolled her eyes. "You must be drunk."

Bill shook his head. He took her hand. "I love you. You're beautiful. And I'm going to keep telling you until you believe me. Got that?"

She just smiled. She worried about the wedding. As happy as she was, she was still upset. She couldn't let on how she felt. The up-and-down emotional ride was exhausting for her.

"We have to decide on what we'll have for dinner, how many people, music, all that," Bill said.

Leah said quietly, "Let's keep it manageable."

Bill smiled. "I agree. I want to spend time with our guests, not just run by everyone and say hello and thank you." Bill held Leah's hand across the table and said, "This will be too special of a day for us not to share our happiness with our good friends. This is something I never thought would happen to me."

At that moment, Nick, the same waiter who met Leah the first night she was at the restaurant, brought dinner to the table. He noticed the ring on Leah's finger. Bill saw him looking at it. Bill had to laugh. He took a deep breath and said, "Yes, Nick, Leah and I will be getting married."

Nick's face broke into a huge, goofy kind of smile.

"Let's see how long it takes for the whole place to know," Bill said and sipped his drink.

"Oh, I won't say anything," Nick said as he put the plates down.

"Like hell you won't," Bill said and laughed. "It's okay."

Nick, still smiling, said, "Oh good, thank you, Bill!"

Bill looked at Leah, who was laughing, then he looked at Nick. Bill rolled his eyes.

Nick walked away to tend to other customers.

Bill was still chuckling. "That kid couldn't keep a lid on it if his life depended on it. I'm surprised he didn't notice the ring when he took our order. He's a good kid." Bill saw Nick stop by and talk to Nancy on his way to another table. "See what I mean?"

"I saw that too." Leah said. They both laughed.

# CHAPTER 4

*Loss and Precious Love*

The next night, they were at the stables visiting Harry. It was a beautiful evening. Leah was hand-grazing Harry, and Bill was grooming him.

"So do you think we can invite Harry to our wedding?" Bill asked.

Leah just looked at him. They both laughed.

Bill's phone rang. "Yes," he said. "Oh, Sara, hello. It's good to hear from you. What's going on?"

There was silence.

"Sara, what?" he said. He listened for a minute. He looked at Leah. "Oh my God."

Leah could tell by the look on Bill's face. "It's Ed, isn't it?"

Bill closed his eyes and nodded his head yes. "She's at the hospital. He didn't make it. He had a massive heart attack."

"Oh God. Let's go," Leah said and walked Harry back to his field. "I'll see you soon, my sweetheart." She kissed his neck, took the halter off, and shut the gate. Leah walked up to Bill, took his hand, and put her head on his arm.

They drove to the hospital in silence. When they saw Sara, she was sitting on a chair in the emergency room, staring into space. Leah went to her immediately. She sat down, put her arms around her, and held her. Bill sat on the other side of them. He hung his head and put his face in his hands. Leah could hear him softly crying.

Bill and Leah stayed close to Sara. They helped her with all the funeral arrangements. After a while, Sara wanted to sell the house. Bill took care of all of that for her, found her a nice retirement community to live in, and moved her in. Bill made sure money was no object. Sara protested, but Bill wouldn't hear of it.

She seemed happy living in a senior environment where she could have friends her own age, friends she could relate to. Bill and Leah visited her regularly and took her places. Sara made friends easily and had a group she hung around with each day.

One day on the way home from a visit with Sara, Bill stopped at a red light and turned to Leah. "I'm worried about Sara. She appears to be doing well, but I can see it in her eyes, you know, how she's really feeling. Thank you for being so willing to help care for her."

"I wouldn't have it any other way, Bill, and you know that," Leah said. She felt so sad. She reached over and held Bill's hand.

As time went by, Bill and Leah continued to notice the sadness in Sara. When questioned, she'd always smile and say she was fine. Her life seemed happy, at least on the outside.

It was a warm Sunday morning, about a month after Ed passed away. Bill and Leah had breakfast at a local diner. "I love having breakfast out," Leah said to Bill as they got into the car. Pancakes are so good when you don't have to clean up."

Bill laughed. "Well, considering how much you ate, if I were cooking, I'd still be in the kitchen."

"Yeah, but they'd be much better," Leah said and hugged him. "I can't wait for our wedding. I hope you like how I look in a wedding dress."

Bill took her hand. "I'll love it. I have no doubts. Nothing can look bad on you."

Sarcastically, Leah said, "Yeah."

"You don't realize how beautiful you are. I see men looking at you. They're wondering what the hell you're doing with someone like me."

Leah got angry. "Stop it. I don't want to hear that. Damn it. Damn all the fools of this earth. They are all just a bunch of fuckers."

This made Bill laugh. He hugged her.

"I know, you love when I cuss," Leah said.

"Well, it makes me laugh," Bill said. "You're such a lady all the time, then you turn around and drop the f-bomb or call someone a—"

Leah stopped him and said, "A fucker. You're damn right! That's 'cause they are and they deserve it," Leah said and checked her face in the mirror on the visor. "Bastards."

Bill laughed.

"It would have been nice if Sara came with us this morning, but I'm glad she has friends that she wants to be with," Leah said.

They pulled into the parking lot of the retirement home. There was an ambulance by the door. Leah sensed something was terribly wrong. She didn't say anything to Bill. They walked in and asked for Sara. The head nurse, who was behind the desk but toward the other end, came over. Leah could tell she had been waiting for them to arrive by the look on her face. She looked at Bill and Leah and in a soft voice said, "I'm so sorry. Sara passed away a short time ago. She was late for breakfast. Her nurse discovered her. I'm so sorry."

Leah could see it in Bill's face. He couldn't process what they had just been told. It was too soon after losing his father-in-law. She could see the blood drain from his face. She held him. "Let's sit down," she said and guided him to a chair. She didn't know what to say.

Leah took out her phone and called Julie. "I need you and Rob now. Sara passed away this morning. Bill is taking it very hard. He's scaring me. We're at the retirement home."

Rob drove Bill and Leah to Bill's. Julie drove Bill's car. "You take care of him. We'll stick around in case you need us," Julie said.

"Okay," Leah replied. "Oh God, I never saw Bill like this."

"Honey, now it's your turn to take care of him," Julie said.

Bill went right to his bedroom and lay down on the bed. He closed his eyes and was very still. Leah sat with him. She rubbed his shoulder. She kissed his cheek. He just lay still. Tears came, and he made no effort to speak. "I'll take care of you," she whispered. "I'll take good care of you, Bill."

He reached over and held her hand. Leah put her head on his chest and held him. "It'll be all right," she whispered. "I promise."

He broke down and sobbed. Leah just held him tight, and they cried.

The next day, Leah went with Bill to the retirement home to clear out Sara's belongings. Bill had a numbness about him. Leah knew not to say too much. Bill took Sara's clothes, odds and ends, and put them in a duffel bag. Leah opened the night table drawer, and there was a picture of Sara's daughter and Bill. It was taken when they were just married and on their honeymoon. On the back there was a handwritten note. "Mom and Dad, thank you for a spectacular wedding. We are so happy and having the time of our lives here in Hawaii. Will see you soon. Love, Sara and Bill."

Sara was absolutely stunning with long blond hair, perfect figure, big dark eyes, perfect features, and an aura about her that was soothing to Leah. There was Bill standing beside her. He had a profound appearance. He was perfectly dressed, had a full head of hair, his handsome face with those wonderful blue eyes and a strong, defined build. Leah wanted to cry but managed not to. How he looked in that picture was how she saw him every day. He was perfect. She somehow managed to hold herself together and not cry. She felt such a deep sadness for Bill. He was the most beautiful man on earth. She loved him so much.

Leah looked at Bill. She could see the emotions in his face, the feelings he couldn't talk about, couldn't put into words. The loss was too great. She walked over to him as he stood by the bed and packed the remaining things Sara had left behind.

"Bill," she said quietly, "I found this in the night table drawer. You might want to hold on to this." And she handed him the picture.

Bill looked at the picture then took it from Leah. He looked at Leah. His face was apologetic. Leah gently touched his hand, looked into his eyes, and smiled at Bill. He tucked the picture away in his wallet. "Thank you for understanding all this," he whispered.

Leah knew Bill would need time to cope. She helped him with the funeral arrangements and accompanied him the day of the funeral. It was very rough on Bill. Leah's heart broke for him. She had no way of consoling him. She felt so helpless, and she knew all she could do was be there for him.

A few days had gone by, and Leah hadn't heard from Bill. While at work, Leah and Macie sat at the front desk, and Leah leaned over and said quietly to Macie, "You know what, Macie, I think Sara died of a broken heart."

Macie looked at Leah. "You're right, and I think Bill thinks so too. It's obvious, Leah."

"I'm very worried about Bill," Leah said quietly. "Do you think I should call him? I haven't called him. I think he needs time alone to deal with this whole thing. What do you think?"

"Leah," Macie said, "you're doing the right thing by giving Bill the space and time he needs. This is very traumatic for him. He told you he never stopped loving his wife. He was part of their family, a son to his wife's parents. They were, in turn, his parents. This whole thing is a very difficult experience for him. I know you know this, but this is losing his parents, and of course it's bringing back the loss of his wife, all those raw emotions that he felt back then. If you are with him, he may feel that he shouldn't be feeling certain things or that he should be concentrating on you. That's the kind of person he is. He needs to take care of his emotional state right now. I think you know what I'm saying. This way, he can deal with things on his own, get to the point where he needs to be to deal with all this, and then he will call. I promise."

Leah shook her head. "I know you're right. It's just he's always there for me. He's so strong, always. In all my craziness, he's there, he doesn't judge me. He understands that he doesn't understand me, but he continues to be there."

"Leah, and now it's your turn." Macie smiled. "You're doing the right thing by giving him the time he needs, and as a result, you are being there for him. He knows you're here, waiting for him to see you. He'll be fine. I promise. Before you know it, he'll be showing up here to bring you home at night."

"Thank you," Leah said. She smiled at Macie. She was so glad to have her for a friend.

For the next few days, Julie gave Leah a ride to and from work. It was a Friday. The rescue was unusually busy. Leah was feeling very frustrated and worried about Bill. The days crept by. Macie saw that

Leah was struggling. She did most of the customer handling. Leah stayed in her office as much as she could to avoid the people who came in. She knew that being in the frame of mind she was, she'd either be fired or end up quitting.

It was about two in the afternoon. Leah had been in her office most of the day. Macie worked the front, Leah only helping when absolutely necessary. Macie came to Leah's office. "Leah, come to the front please."

Leah was in a foul mood. "What the hell for now?" she said. She realized how she sounded. "I'm sorry. What do you need?"

"Just come up, please," Macie said and walked away.

Leah threw her pen down, put her phone in her purse, and walked up front. There, on her side of the front desk, was a beautiful bouquet of wildflowers. It was huge, and lying on the side of the vase was a purple rose. She just stared at it. Of course, Kallie and all the kids began to come up front once word got out that Leah had flowers delivered to her. Leah took the card off the bouquet. She read it, unaware that she was reading it out loud. "Leah, thank you for being you. I will love you always. I can't make it without you." Leah looked up, and saw all the kids in the room with her. Macie, along with all of them, was smiling.

Kallie said, "That's beautiful, but I don't get the purple rose."

Leah smiled. "A purple rose means love at first sight."

Kallie smiled and said, "Wow, this is the kind of love I hope I find in my lifetime."

That night, Leah and Macie were closing up the office. Kallie was helping, since it was later than usual due to how busy it was.

Leah was locking the cash drawer. She turned around, and Bill was standing in the lobby. "Ready?" he asked. He looked at her and smiled.

Leah had the biggest smile on her face. She looked into his eyes and said, "Yes, I'm ready."

Kallie put her arm around Leah and said, "Have a good night." Kallie looked at Bill and nodded.

Macie waked over to her and whispered, "I told you, honey. Have fun tonight."

"We will, thank you," Leah said. She walked over to Bill, took his hand, and they left.

Kallie gathered up the bouquet and the rose. She smiled and said to Macie, "I'll put this on her desk so she can get all goofy again in the morning." They both laughed. "I don't know the details, but I know it's complicated, and they need each other." Her eyes watered, and she then said, "I meant what I said. I hope I find a love like that before I die."

Macie smiled at Kallie and said, "For someone as young as you are, you're very observant, Kallie. They are a unique couple, that's for sure. There's a strong bond between them. They are two very complicated lives that came together just in time. I wish I had had that kind of love in my life. Not going to happen now. It's nice to see two people love each other the way they do."

It was chilly out. "You don't have a jacket," Bill said and put his arm around Leah as they approached his car. He said, "They knew?"

Leah looked at him. "They knew about your in-laws' passing away and that you were hurting, and so was I. They were all worried about you. Everyone carried my load at work when I just couldn't deal with it. Some of the things we deal with on a daily basis are so hard, and I was so worried about you, I couldn't deal with it at times. That's what we do at my job. I'm pretty lucky if you ask me."

Bill smiled. He opened the car door. "How about we visit Harry and then we can go get a pizza, have some wine, talk, hold hands—"

"I'd love that," Leah said softly. "Are you all right? Bill, I was so worried."

"What, that I wouldn't come back to you?" he asked with a sad tone in his voice.

"No, no, I was just worried about you. This must have been so hard for you. I can't even imagine how you are feeling. I never knew how it felt to belong in a family that knew the meaning of family and what loving a family is all about."

Bill started the car. "Thank you for giving me the time I needed to be alone. Besides losing my wife, and almost losing you when you"—he stopped, took a deep breath—"this was a real rough one for me. I was even surprised at how it made me feel." He paused for a second and then said, "I have a present for you."

She smiled. "What?"

"You can have it when we get to the barn. Decide if you'd like to go to that little Italian restaurant we like or bring the pizza home." Bill laughed.

"What are you laughing at?" Leah asked.

"The look on your face when I said you can have your present at the barn," Bill said and pulled out of the parking lot.

"Well, that's not fair," Leah said, laughing. "I think I want a salad, bread, sautéed broccoli, a pizza, extra large with peppers, onions, and red wine."

They were stopped at a traffic light. Bill looked over at her. "By any chance, are you hungry? And you want red?"

"Yes, and yes, red. I'm feeling very bold tonight, and very good, like I am part of things."

"Rob was right, I guess," Bill said and laughed. "I love you, Leah. I really do."

"Okay, then what did you get me?" Leah asked. "Why can't I have it now?"

"Because I want to make you sweat," Bill said with a childish smile on his face.

"It's too damn cold to sweat," Leah said and she had to laugh. 'C'mon, what is it?"

Bill just laughed. "You'll see." And he refused to look at her or talk about it.

"Damn it," Leah said.

This made Bill laugh harder.

"Oh shut up," she said, and looked out the window.

Bill reached over and held her hand.

When they got to the barn, Bill no sooner turned the car off when Leah said, "Okay, can I have it?"

Bill leaned over and kissed her.

"Not that!" Leah said.

Bill laughed. "Okay, close your eyes."

"Oh brother," Leah said and rolled her eyes.

"Close 'em," Bill said.

Leah sighed. "All right," she said and shut her eyes.

Bill got out and opened the back door to the car. "You stay there." He came back to the front. "Okay, open your eyes." Leah opened her eyes, and he handed her a box. It was wrapped in plain brown paper.

She looked at him and opened it. When she saw what was inside, she laughed. "You are a riot!" she said. "This is great!"

"Do you like it?" Bill asked.

"Are you kidding me? What did you do? And how did you get these?" Leah looked through the box. "I can't believe this. You actually got me *Gunsmoke* radio programs?"

"Well, yeah," Bill said. "We can ride around and listen to them. It'll be fun and something different to do."

Leah smiled at him. "Thank you so much!"

"Oh, and I have something else for you," Bill said and reached over and opened the glove compartment. He pulled out a small box wrapped in gold paper with a gold ribbon on it.

"This is also for you," he said as he handed her the box.

Leah just looked at him. She opened it very carefully. When she opened the box, there was a beautiful necklace with a small horse head, his neck arched with a mane made of white gold and diamonds. She didn't know what to say. Leah stared at it for a few minutes. "It's so beautiful. You shouldn't have."

Bill looked at her in a way he hadn't ever before. Leah looked into those eyes of his, and again they took her breath away. "Yes, I should have. Let me put it on you."

Leah gently took it out of the box and handed it to Bill. She turned around so he could clasp it. She turned and looked at Bill. She put her arms around his neck and kissed him gently on his lips. "Thank you. You are so sweet."

Bill smiled. He said, "I know how being in the country with your horse makes you feel. I can see it in your eyes. You feel completely at peace, like you are part of things, like you belong, not out of place when you're dealing with the world. It's very obvious in your eyes, Leah. Even with me, which I wish wasn't true. I'm trying to understand, and to help. So wear this and always know you are beautiful, Leah, and know you do belong, and be at peace. You are my world." Bill smiled and said, "C'mon, Harry's waiting for us."

Leah wore the necklace every day from then on.

The next day, Julie picked Leah up for work. Leah had the necklace on. When she got in Julie's car, the sun caught the diamonds. Julie couldn't believe how beautiful it was. "Leah, oh my God, what a beautiful necklace!"

Leah smiled. "Bill gave it to me last night. I can't believe it myself. Julie, I'm so happy. He told me to wear it, so I feel at peace that I belong, the way I do when I'm with my horse in the country. Julie, I am so in love with this man. He doesn't have a clue about me, yet he does all this and accepts me for the crazy bitch I am."

Julie looked at Leah. "So doesn't that tell you how he feels about you? Few people in this world get that from another human being. He accepts you just as you are. What more do you want?"

"He doesn't accept me as I am because he doesn't know me as I am, and I want to be as beautiful as he thinks I am. I want to drop my clothes in front of him and have him scoop me up in his arms and make love to me. Instead, he'll run and leave me like a bad nightmare." She laughed in a sarcastic tone and said, "*Nightmare* is such an appropriate word for me."

"Leah," Julie said in a calm tone. "I wish I had the answers for you, but I don't."

"Julie," Leah said, "neither do I. So whatever happens, happens. I won't leave him, but he will discard me for sure on our wedding night. Isn't there a twenty-four-hour time period where you can get out of any contract? Or is it forty-eight?" Leah had a funny look on her face, and Julie became concerned.

"What are you thinking?" Julie asked with caution in her voice.

"Nothing. I'm going to let it all play out." Leah's mood changed on a dime, as it often did. Julie knew better than to challenge it. "Bill and I were talking about our wedding, and we were wondering if we could have it in your yard, since we met at your place…"

Julie interrupted. "Are you kidding? I was going to insist because what could be more romantic? Yes, of course. We have to find you the perfect dress. Perfect flowers…"

Leah smiled. "Yes, I know. I want purple roses. Lots of purple roses mixed in with red, yellow, and pink roses."

Julie smiled. "Oh, love at first sight is the theme?"

Leah laughed. "Yes, how did you know? About purple roses I mean."

"Well, when we were at your place for Bill's birthday, you had two purple roses on the table. I had no idea why. I looked it up. Leah, how beautiful of an idea."

"Julie, I told you the minute I saw Bill, I knew." Leah paused. "There was just something special about him. It definitely was love at first sight."

Julie smiled. "I know. I remember how you went on and on about him."

"Bill is the best thing that ever happened to me, Julie. I'm so glad that—"

Julie again finished her sentence. "You came to my party. And you're glad you met Bill…and didn't—"

Leah laughed. "Yes. Okay? Satisfied? I'm glad I came to your party and met Bill. Let's leave it at that for now and not spoil the way I'm feeling."

Julie hugged Leah. "It'll all work out. I'll take you to look at wedding dresses tonight after work, okay?"

"I'd like that. I want something simple but elegant and pretty," Leah said. "I want to knock Bill off his feet when he sees me walk to him on our wedding day. Then he can leave me in the dust at night."

Julie patted Leah's hand. After taking a deep breath so she wouldn't argue with Leah, she said, "Not to worry, you've already knocked him off his feet. You're the only one who doesn't know it yet. Do you want to do the bridal shop thing or not? What exactly do you want? Or don't you know yet?"

Leah let out a big sigh. "I'm not totally sure. I want something white, that's okay, isn't it?"

Julie laughed. "Whatever you want is all right. I am so glad this is happening. I told you so many times how much we love Bill. He is so special. And you, well, you know how we feel about you. You both deserve to be together and happy forever."

Leah didn't answer. She just looked at Julie and smiled.

"Stop worrying," Julie said. "So what will it be? Bridal shop or mall?"

"I'm not a bridal-shop person. Let's go to the mall. What I'm looking for won't be in a bridal shop," Leah said.

They pulled up to the rescue. "Okay, I'll be here at seven for you," Julie said.

"Can you make it at six? I can scoot out early today. Macie will cover. She's taking an evening off next week, so she said she'd cover me one night."

"Six it is," Julie said and smiled. "Hopefully we can catch up with Bill and Rob after we shop. Maybe at Bill's restaurant and get a drink and something to snack on. What'd you think?"

"That sounds great. I'll call Bill and let him know I'll be with you after work, and see if he'll be at the restaurant tonight." Leah got out of the car. "Thanks again, Julie. See you later."

Six o'clock seemed to take forever to roll around. Finally, it was time to leave work and shop for Leah's wedding dress. Julie and Leah walked through the mall. Leah hadn't found anything she really liked.

"I'm getting discouraged, Julie," Leah said.

"Oh stop. That perfect dress is just waiting for you to buy it." They walked into one of the larger, nicer stores.

"I hope you're right," Leah said, "because this is the last store I'm going in. I'll get married in slacks and a shirt, with my flip-flops and call it a day if I have to."

"Oh, someone's getting cranky," Julie said as they got to the dress department. "Let's split up. I'll look at one end, you at the other, and we'll meet in the middle. Okay?"

Leah smiled and nodded. "I hate shopping."

"Be quiet," Julie said as they split up to shop. They took their time. This was the last store in the mall to shop for a wedding dress. It was getting late.

"Julie," Leah called, "I think I found it. If it fits…"

When Julie came over, Leah was holding the dress. It was white, with a cape-like collar over the shoulders. It had pastel flowers with small scattered rhinestones on some of the petals. There were four purple roses in the pattern.

"What do you think?" Leah asked Julie.

"I think it's perfect. Absolutely perfect. Try it on." Julie smiled. She had the feeling that this was the dress for Leah.

When Leah came out of the dressing room, Julie just stared at her. The dress fit her like it had been made just for her. It fell loosely over her body. It was cut just low enough to be elegant.

"I'm glad it's not tight." Leah said.

"I said it's perfect, Leah. You look like a dream. Bill won't believe how beautiful you look," Julie said.

Leah and Julie got to the restaurant around ten thirty. Leah began to get anxious. Too much reality was settling in. She began to panic. You go in first," Leah said to Julie. "I'll be right in."

Julie just looked at her. She knew what she was thinking. Saying nothing, she got out of the car. "I'll wait for you in the lobby."

Leah took her water from her purse and swallowed a piece of candy. She hated herself, but hated the panic, anxiety, and depression even more. She wondered how it was even possible to have these feelings. All she wanted was to be a normal woman. She began to panic about the wedding. Soon, the candy would calm her and the wine she will have will take it all away, at least for a while. She got out of the car and walked into the restaurant to meet Julie.

Nancy was at the front. She broke into a huge smile when Leah walked in to meet Julie. As Julie and Leah walked toward the bar, Nancy said, "Bill and Rob are waiting for you in the bar. Leah, congratulations on your wedding."

Julie and Leah turned and Leah said, "Thank you, Nancy."

Rob and Bill were talking. Bill was very candid and out of character this night. He said to Rob, "You know the girls are looking for a wedding dress."

Rob nodded, "Yeah, Julie told me that's why they were shopping."

"Well, I'm wondering, I've been wondering for a while now, about how she'll take it on our wedding night. You know, I'm—"

Rob looked at Bill and interrupted him. "You are exactly who she loves and wants to be with for the rest of her life."

Bill took the picture of himself and Sara from his wallet. "This is what she should be getting. I'm embarrassed to even expect her to be with me. She's so beautiful. Leah found this when we were cleaning out Sara's room, and handed it to me. She never said a word, never blinked an eye. She just, well, she—"

Rob looked at the picture and finished the sentence for Bill. "Well, she just loves you, Bill, and the man in that picture is what she's getting." He put his hand on Bill's shoulder. "Leah is a fragile person in many ways, but not when it comes to what and especially who she loves. She wouldn't be here if you weren't the man she loves. We've known her for a very long time, and she's a tough one regardless of what makes her as fragile as fine crystal sometimes."

Bill tucked the picture back in his wallet. He smiled at Rob and said quietly, "Thanks." Leah's anxiety was beginning to set in. Her chest started to pound and her head to spin. Leah and Julie walked into the bar, and Rob and Bill were at a table near the window. It was one of those tables with the tall stools. Bill tuned and saw them. He got up and met them. "Hello, you two." He put his arm around Leah. She loved when he did that. She felt so safe. Safe from herself and the world.

Leah smiled. She put her arm around him as they walked to the table. "You look great tonight!" Not knowing the conversation he had just had with Rob, this made him feel good. Leah noticed he seemed exceptionally glad to receive the compliment. "What?" Leah asked.

Bill just smiled. "Nothing. I'm glad to see you tonight. I ordered some things for us. I know you're probably starved."

"Of course, I am. Shopping isn't my thing. But I did find a gorgeous dress for our wedding. I hope you'll like it," Leah said as she and Julie sat down.

A glass of red wine was waiting for Leah and Julie. Leah took a huge sip of hers.

"I took the liberty of getting you red tonight," Bill said. "I hope you don't mind. I thought you could use it after shopping." He laughed. "We all know how you hate it."

Julie laughed. "Oh boy, you have no idea. She is a royal bitch when she shops."

"You are a hundred percent right," Leah said as she took a big sip and then set the glass down. "I am a royal bitch when I shop. And yes, red wine is perfect after a night of shopping."

The food had just arrived: fried shrimp, onion rings, chicken strips, french fries, and fresh broccoli. Enough to feed an army. Or at least Leah.

"Oh boy, how'd you know? And you kept it balanced with the broccoli," Leah said to Bill.

"Rob and I just know what you two like this time of night," Bill said and sipped his drink.

"Well, I'm going to have some of everything." Leah took a plate and began to pile it on.

"Rob, Julie, you better get your share quick," Bill said. "I may have to order seconds at this rate." He looked at Leah and smiled at her.

They ate and talked well into the night. Leah felt good.

Bill drove her home, of course. Leah was looking at Bill as they pulled up to her house.

"What's wrong?" Bill asked.

She just smiled and said, "Oh, nothing is wrong. I just love you so much. You are so beautiful. You make me feel so good."

Bill smiled. He got out, opened her door, and as she got out of the car he put his hand around her waist to guide her and walked her into the house. Remembering his conversation with Rob earlier in the night, and also the one when he asked why she doesn't get help, he took her hand as they stood in the living room and said, "Leah, if you ever want me to help you with anything…"

Leah asked, "What do you mean?"

"Oh, just anything," Bill said, trying not to sound obvious.

Leah wasn't sure what he meant, but she thought it may be related to money. "Bill, I've never asked anyone for help in my entire life, and I'm not going to start now. I've been and done it all alone all my life, and I don't need anything except to be loved. And I would never ask you for money."

Bill looked at her. At that point, Ricky and Honey had made their way over to Leah and Bill and were begging for attention. Bill had to laugh. "Okay, kids, let's sit on the couch for a few minutes." Bill sat down, and Ricky jumped up beside him,

Leah handed Honey to Bill. "I'll get something for us to drink, and if you'd like, we can watch some bad TV for a while."

"That would be nice, thanks," Bill said as he played with the dogs.

Leah came into the living room with a glass of wine for herself and a Jack Daniel's for Bill. She put them on the coffee table and said, "Okay, kids, move it. He's mine."

Ricky reluctantly got off the couch. Leah took Honey from Bill and put her in her bed. She threw a look at Leah. Bill laughed. "Oh boy, if looks could kill!"

Leah laughed. "I know. I always tell her she looks like Bette Davis when she does that."

Bill laughed. "They aren't spoiled, are they?"

Leah got on the couch and cuddled next to Bill. She had the TV remote in her hands and was scrolling through the channels. Being so late, not much was on but reruns. She stopped abruptly. "Yay! A crime show from the seventies. Is this okay?"

'Sure, whatever you like." Bill put his arm around her. They watched together.

"So did you ever notice how, like right now, the top is down on the convertible, and the PI he's driving like a bat out of hell, his hair is perfect. Can you explain that?" Leah said.

Bill laughed. "No, I can't. All I know is they slicked their hair down back in the day."

"Okay, so what about the guy who's always in the back seat when the PI goes into a building and then comes out to the car? He drives away, and some hoodlum pops up in the back with a gun and demands all kinds of crazy things or else. A PI should know to lock the car, damn it."

"Leah, you have too much time on your hands," Bill said and laughed. He hugged her, and then said, "And yes, I have noticed. Too funny. Is this how we'll spend our late nights when we're married?"

Leah looked up at him. "Is something wrong with that?" she said and giggled.

"Oh, no, of course not," Bill said and took a big sip of his drink.

"You obviously know the right answer," Leah said.

Bill made a funny face and didn't say a word.

Leah patted his shoulder, and he knew the right answer was no answer,

It was getting close to four thirty in the morning. Leah finally fell asleep while leaning on Bill. He looked at her face. He loved her so much. He brushed her hair away from her face. He got up very gently so as not to wake her. He took Ricky and Honey out. He had to lift Honey, which he had only done a few times. It was funny how she seemed to know he wasn't sure of himself. She stood patiently until he got a good grip on her. When he came in, Leah was still sound asleep. Bill put Honey gently in her bed, and Ricky lay down on the couch with Leah as he always did. Bill went to Leah's bedroom and took her pillow from her bed and the shawl she kept on the end of the bed. He gently put the pillow under her head. He covered her with the shawl. Then, he went into the kitchen and got the coffee pot ready for morning. He set the timer. He put a cup by the coffee maker. He looked around for a piece of paper and a pen. He found one under the microwave counter. He wrote, "Leah, good night, sweetheart. You fell fast asleep, just when the hoodlum popped up in the back seat. The PI managed to save himself yet again. You look so beautiful when you sleep. Like an angel. I took the kids out and set the coffee for you. Pleasant dreams. I will see you tomorrow. Love you, Bill." He slipped the note carefully under the wineglass on the coffee table. "Good night, kids," he whispered to the dogs. They looked up at him. The cats were sleeping on the back of the couch. They never opened their eyes. He straightened the necklace that Leah wore every day since he gave it to her, so it wouldn't get tangled in her sleep. Bill leaned over and kissed Leah on her cheek and left.

# CHAPTER 5

## *Alone/Dreams/Reality*

The day before the wedding.

Leah was going to have dinner at Bill's tonight. She was getting anxious. She sat on her bed knowing what would happen tomorrow night. She would be alone in the end. Leah began to cry. She opened her dresser drawer.

"Let's just set this up now," Leah said to herself and she took out a full bottle of pills and set them on her dresser. Then, Leah went to the kitchen. She got a glass and opened a bottle of wine. She put the cork in the bottle and wiped her face. She took a napkin from the table and brought everything to her bedroom. She set things up neatly on her dresser and sat on her bed. Ricky came to the bedroom and sat on the bed and put his head in her lap. Leah just rubbed his head. Honey couldn't climb the stairs. She looked up the steps and sat patiently at the bottom. Leah said to Ricky, "I'm sorry, kiddo. Julie will be over to take care of all of you after we supposedly leave for our honeymoon." Leah sighed. "She'll find me, be mad as hell at me, but she'll forgive me and take very good care of you guys. She always wanted a horse anyway, and a couple of dogs and cats. I'll watch over you from heaven…if God lets me in." Leah leaned over and hugged Ricky and cried and cried. "I'll be gone in a matter of minutes. I just can't take this any longer. I don't want to leave any of you, but I just can't go on. When Bill turns me away." She put her hands on her face. "Oh God."

Leah held Ricky for a while. She began to calm down. She accepted her decision and was not going to back out this time. "I'm at peace with all this. I'm not at peace with living like this anymore. I'm finished."

Leah got up and looked in the mirror. "Ugh…" she said. She looked at the clock on the dresser. "Ricky, Bill will be here soon for me. I have to fix my face so he doesn't know I was crying. And I have to change these clothes. I will see you tonight." Leah got herself together, fixed her hair and her face. "Better," she said to Ricky. She closed the bedroom door, and they both went downstairs. Honey was still at the bottom of the steps. Leah just smiled at her. "You precious little thing," she said to her. She knelt down and hugged her. Honey wagged her tail. "I'll see you tonight. We'll sit on the couch and watch TV all night." She kissed her gently on her forehead, picked her up, hugged her, and put her in her bed. "I love you so much," Leah whispered in her ear. "You have changed my life for the better in so many ways. Julie will take great care of you, I promise."

Bill and Leah got to Bill's house at five. He put his key in the door. The door wouldn't open at first, so he struggled for a short while before it opened. "Well, that never happened before," Bill said. He turned to Leah and took her hand. He held her hand tight, as he led her through the door. She smiled at him. He looked into her eyes. Her heart melted, as it always did when he looked at her. He walked her inside.

"Bill," Leah whispered, "I feel a little light-headed."

Bill just looked at her. "So do I, slightly." He put his hand around Leah's waist and held her for a second. "'Must be all that's going on. I'll start dinner. Come into the kitchen and keep me company." Leah sat at a small table in the kitchen. Of course, the kitchen was a gourmet kitchen with anything a chef could want or need to make a fabulous meal. For a while, they were quiet. Leah watched Bill get things ready, and as he cooked, she smiled.

Bill looked at her and said, "I'm feeling better, are you?"

She nodded. "Yes, I am. I think you're right. So much is happening. All of it is very nice, though."

Bill smiled and said, "What are you thinking? You're looking at me sort of funny."

Leah just smiled, but she worried about the wedding night. She wouldn't say that to him. "I'm just thinking about how much I love you and how cute you are in the kitchen."

Bill laughed. "I love you too, Leah. Always will. I'm not sure that I'm cute in the kitchen, though."

She smiled, but thought to herself how the love affair would abruptly end. There was nothing she could do at this point. Things had gone too far. The reality was that she lied without saying a word. She was everything and everyone she hated. She despises liars. She knew Bill loved her, but he didn't know her. He had never seen her. He never asked her for more than a kiss, to hold her hand and a hug. He was so respectful of her. He was such a gentleman.

"Excuse me for a minute. I have to check my face," Leah said and stood up. "I'll be right back." She went to the bathroom and shut the door. She took her bottle of water from her purse and a piece of candy. She'd start to feel better soon. The anxiety would soon lessen. It wouldn't leave, but she'd be able to contain it at least. "I hate myself," she said to herself while looking in the mirror.

When she got back to the kitchen, Bill had put a glass of wine on the table. "How'd you know?" she said, smiled, and took a sip.

Bill smiled at her. "I know that look by now, Leah."

Leah's heart felt heavy. "Thank you."

Bill went over to her, kissed her cheek, and said, "I hope you like what I'm making."

Leah just watched Bill as he prepared dinner. He was so confident in the kitchen. No wonder his restaurant was such a success. "Whatever you're making will be great."

Leah and Bill finished dinner. Bill sipped his wine. Leah gulped hers down and went for more. Bill, as always, never said a word to her about it. He accepted her. She knew that.

Then, he looked at her and she knew what he wanted. She shared his desire, but wouldn't dare initiate it. How could she? She was afraid. She thought of the bottle of wine and pills she had set up for tomorrow, when she came in the house, after their first night together, alone and revolted with herself. She was glad she thought to set things up a day early. The pain would now end a day early. In a way she was relieved. It'd finally be over, and maybe she'd find peace. She thought she might go straight to hell for taking her life, but she also believed she was in hell as she lived. She thought to herself, *What's the difference?*

She looked into Bill's eyes. "I have nothing to change into," she said.

Bill softly said to Leah, "You can put one of my robes on. Although you'll drown in it. You can take one from the closet in my room."

They hadn't gotten up from the table yet. Leah was almost paralyzed with fear. Bill looked deep into her eyes. He slightly smiled, but was sad. He laughed a little then said, "You know, it's okay if you can't do this. I understand. You've never been with a man"—he stumbled for words for the first time since Leah knew him—"like me, have you?"

She looked at him. She couldn't speak at first. She knew what he meant. She felt terrible that he'd even think this way. Leah understood only too well as her issues were so far worse than his. She just kept staring at Bill's face, his beautiful face. A tear fell on her cheek. She hurt for him. She never looked at Bill that way, not even for a second. Leah remembered Julie asking her the night of the party would Bill's size bother her. Of course not. She loved him. Completely. Unconditionally.

No, Leah had never been with a corpulent man. That didn't matter to her at all. She loved him as he was. He was the best thing that ever happened to her. Bill was her hero. The part that hurt her so much was that he thought he loved her as she was, with all her crazy behaviors, her depression, her ups and downs…one minute laughing, the next, crying, the attempts to and wanting to die. Because she wasn't honest with Bill, he didn't know her at all. Her guilt was strangling her.

At this point, Leah realized she now had her way out of the humiliation, the rejection she'd get and righteously so. Her brain was spinning. She could back out now, walk away from this man who she loved so much and so deeply. She could, at this moment, avoid all the hurt she'd face and deserved. She loved him with her entire being. Leah looked into his eyes. She couldn't do it. She decided she would let him be the one to let her go so she wouldn't break his heart as it has been broken before by life's cruel jokes. Bill would realize she lied to him without saying a word, but to end the relationship had to be his decision. She couldn't be the cause of his hurt, although she knew she would be anyway, because she deceived him in her silence. Her heart felt as if it were crumbling inside of her.

Leah managed to smile. She wiped a tear from her face, took a breath, and said, "No, I've never been with a man like you. A man who loves me unconditionally and as much as you do. I've never been with a man that I love as much as I love you, Bill. I never knew I could feel this way because of another human being."

He took her hand and they went to his bedroom.

She became sick to think of the end result. She felt robbed that the end would come a day early, after such a nice evening with the man she loved. She wanted every second possible with this man, whom she loved so deeply.

This was the end of the relationship for Leah with Bill. Leah was positive of it. She couldn't shake the panic that was setting in. She had never been with a man like Bill, but little did he know she was the one who he'd never been with. Surely, he would discard her immediately. She is so repulsive, so disgusting, so ugly. She wished, as she so often did, that she'd drop to the ground, dead. She had to go through with this now that the wedding would be tomorrow. Now she knew. There'd be no wedding.

Leah opened the closet and took out a blue robe. Bill smiled at her and said, "Go into the bathroom and change."

The bathroom was huge and elegant. She kept the lights off. She cried because this was the end of her dream. Bill's robe hung on the door. There was a huge skylight in the bathroom. The moonlight shone through and lit the entire room on its own. She hated the light. She loved the dark because it let her be who she wasn't, who she'd never be again. Leah proceeded to take off her clothes, sickened by herself. She looked down at herself, in the beam of light the moon provided against her will. She stared at herself. She was normal, not mutilated, not someone who could sicken the devil. Leah couldn't understand what happened. She was as she was in her early twenties. She wiped the tears from her face, put on the robe, and went into Bill's bedroom, not knowing what to expect after this. She was so confused. She felt weak.

Bill was lying in bed, totally covered. He laughed quietly when she walked into the bedroom.

"What's funny?" Leah asked.

"You in that robe." He smiled at her.

She sat on the edge of the bed, next to Bill. She was ready to give herself to him, but what was going on? She looked at herself again, and she was normal still. She stood up, turned, and looked at Bill and dropped the robe to the floor. Bill looked at her.

He whispered to her, "Leah, you're so beautiful."

She slowly got into the bed, under the covers with him. She reached out and touched him. He was so strong and was how she saw him in that picture in his days past. Leah kissed his lips. "Bill, I love you."

He began to gently touch her shoulders. His touch made her feel so loved and beautiful. She was warm from deep down inside.

She looked at him again, and there he was, the man she met at the party a little over a year ago, and has been with all this time. The man she loved so very much. The man who loved her too. She gently ran her hands over him. Bill smiled at Leah. He drew her near and softly kissed her lips. Bill's touch was gentle. Leah caressed him, kissed him. He kissed her and held her softly. She felt so complete, so peaceful, so loved. She could hardly believe all this. As they held each other, they kissed again and became one.

# CHAPTER 6

## Complete Love/Peace

Julie and Rob were sitting on the couch together and were having a drink while watching the news. "I can't believe the wedding is tomorrow. It sure came up fast," Julie said. She got off the couch. "I'll be right back." She walked into the kitchen to put her glass in the sink.

"Holy cow!" Rob said out loud.

"What?" Julie said and came back to the living room.

"Look at this pileup on the freeway. Oh my God! This happened sometime late this afternoon around five, they said," Rob said.

"Oh my God is right," Julie said. "You take your life into your hands these days when you get in your car."

"Look, the caption says only two people died, though. A miracle for sure. A man and a woman, burned beyond recognition. They were hit from behind and thrown into the crash. Holy shit!" Rob said and finished his drink. He continued to read the caption. He shook his head. "So sad. I hope, for the family's sake, they can ID them sooner rather than later."

Julie had a sarcastic smile on her face. "Maybe Leah is right. We watch too much news. It's all bad or so it seems."

The wedding day.

Leah and Julie were in Julie's bedroom and Julie was helping Leah get ready to walk down the aisle. Julie looked at Leah in a serious way. "Maybe I shouldn't say this, but I have to. I expected a phone call from you last night, panicking about today. You look different today. That look of panic and uneasiness in your eye is gone, Leah. You look like you are at total peace with things and completely happy today."

Leah looked at Julie and hugged her. "I can't explain it, but I am." Leah looked into Julie's eyes. "Last night, Bill asked me to—"

Julie knew immediately what Leah meant. She said softly, before Leah could finish her sentence, "That's sort of what I was worried about last night."

Leah smiled and her eyes filled with tears. "I was so frightened. I knew it would be the end of me and Bill. I was ready to accept it, and then, well, and then I planned on finishing it all. I was too exhausted to fight it all any longer. I had everything set up for when I basically ran home from our wedding night so I could just be done with all of it." Leah took a deep breath. "I don't know what happened, but when I looked at myself last night, before I went to Bill, I was normal, Julie, as normal as I was when I was young. He told me I was beautiful." A tear fell from her face. She wiped it off quickly. "I don't want to ruin my face," she said and smiled. "I love him so much, Julie. He tells me I'm beautiful all the time. Last night was so special. I'll never forget it. I can't wait to be his wife."

Julie was equally confused, but didn't question what Leah said. She just smiled at Leah and said, "I'm so happy for both of you. C'mon, let's get out there. Your man is waiting."

Leah smiled and nodded. Leah took one last look in the mirror and adjusted the horse necklace that Bill had given her. She smiled.

Leah and Julie walked out of the house into the backyard, holding each other by the arm. Their guests eagerly awaited this wedding. All the guests knew the depth of this love that Leah and Bill had for each other. Leah looked up, and there he was, that magnificent man she met that night at Julie's party, standing there, in a black-and-white tuxedo, waiting for her to walk to him to become his wife. She whispered, "He looks so strong, so handsome, so perfect."

Julie whispered back, "That's because he is." They both smiled and giggled.

Rob was with Bill. They were standing by the Preacher. Rob walked over to Leah as Julie walked ahead to Bill. She hugged Bill and kissed him on his cheek and stood with him while Rob took Leah's arm and began to walk her to Bill.

The preacher stood before Leah and Bill and began the ceremony.

"Welcome, ladies and gentlemen. We have gathered here today to witness the uniting in marriage of Leah and Bill.

"They are taking the first step in their new beginning, their new life together. The ability and desire for one human being to love another is perhaps the most precious and fulfilling gift that has been entrusted to us. Loving someone is to look into the soul of your beloved and accept what you see. It is the ultimate commitment that challenges humans to become all that we are meant to be. Each of you brings gifts to the other today. Gifts of hope and laughter, focus and seriousness, sensitivity and recognition of the beautiful and profound.

"Love is patient and kind. Love is not jealous or boastful, or proud or rude. It does not demand its own way. It is not irritable and it keeps no records of being wronged. Love never gives up, never loses faith.

"Let us pray: Our Father, we come today as family, friends, those who are physically present and those whom we love who are now with you, asking your blessings upon these two lives. You have made us so that we are incomplete without each other, so that we yearn for someone whom we can love and whose love we can receive.

"We pray that when joy comes, may they share it together. We pray that when sorrow threatens, may they bear it together. In gladness or in tears, in sunshine or shadows, may they ever draw closer to each other and nearer to you in the eternal triangle."

The preacher paused, smiled, and said, "Bill and Leah have vows they have written."

Bill looked at Leah. He smiled at her. He took a deep breath. He took a gentle hold of Leah's hands and began his vows. "Leah, do you remember our first date when we had the radio on in my car, and you asked me to stop at a radio station so you could listen to that song, 'This Guy's in Love with You'? And then you said you hoped, ever since you were eleven years old, that someone could feel that way about you someday?" Bill paused, looked into her eyes and continued, "Well, that's how I felt about you from the minute I saw you. You stole my heart. I fell in love with you right then." He put his hand on his heart and said, "I'm in love with you, Leah. I'm so in love with you that there are no words to say how much." He ran his hand through her hair and kissed her on her cheek.

Leah couldn't believe what she just heard. She stared at him. Before beginning her vows, she said softly, "I can't believe you remembered that." Bill smiled at her. She was so happy. While they still held hands, Leah began to say her vows. "When I met you that night, right here at the party, I looked at you and fell head over heels, deeply in love with you. From that second on, my heart has belonged to you. I'm not sure how or why I got to be the luckiest girl on earth to have you, but I'm so glad I am. You don't know me, yet you do. You accept me in all that I do, and you continue to love me. You give me unconditional love. For years my days and nights were nothing but sadness, pain, and loneliness. You are what is meant when someone speaks of magic. I used to think that word wasn't about something real." She paused for a second, smiled at Bill, and continued, "Now I know different. Magic is about you. I love you."

Tears fell on Julie's cheeks. Rob fought tears. Bill looked at Leah. His eyes said all she needed to know.

The preacher began to speak. "Bill, do you take Leah to be your lawfully wedded wife, to love and cherish, from this day forward, for better or worse, for richer or poorer, in sickness and in health for as long as you both shall live?"

Bill said softly, "I do."

The preacher looked at Leah. "Leah, do you take Bill to be your lawfully wedded husband, to love and cherish, from this day forward, for better or worse, for richer or poorer, in sickness and in health for as long as you both shall live?"

Leah responded with a smile on her face, "I do."

The preacher smiled and said, "May I have the rings?" Rob handed them to him. "Though small in size, these rings are very large in significance. Made of precious metal, they remind us that love is never cheap nor common. Made in a circle, their design tells us that love must never come to an end: we must keep it continuous.

"As you wear these rings, whether together or far apart, may they be a constant reminder of these promises that are made today.

"Now, Bill, repeat after me:

"With this ring, I give you my heart. I promise from this day forward you will never walk alone. May my heart be your shelter and my arms be your home."

Bill repeated every word. His voice was strong and solid. He looked at Leah. His heart held hers deep within him. Leah felt so warm, so protected, so lucky to have this man as her husband. As she looked at him, she thought to herself, *He is so beautiful. So perfect.* Bill slipped the ring on her finger. His hands, so big and safe. Leah smiled.

The preacher looked at Leah. "Leah, repeat after me." She nodded.

The preacher began, "With this ring, I give you my heart. I promise from this day forward you will never walk alone. May my heart be your shelter and my arms be your home."

Leah looked at Bill and recited the words. He looked at her, and her heart skipped a beat. Leah put Bill's ring on his finger. She felt as if she was in a dream, but knew all this was very real.

The preacher said, "I now pronounce you man and wife. Bill, you may kiss your bride." Just at that moment, two lightning bugs flew by Leah and Bill. They both saw them and looked at each other. They giggled at the same time. Bill's eyes sparkled. Leah couldn't believe how beautiful all this was.

The preacher smiled and declared, "Ladies and gentlemen, it is my honor to introduce to you for the first time, Mr. and Mrs. Bill Stone!"

Their guests cheered so loud and clapped.

Bill looked at Leah. She was radiant. He held her gently, as he always had. She put her arms around his shoulders. They looked at each other, taking in every second of this special moment. They kissed. Their love was solid between them, a true and complete love, unique and with a depth only they could know.

Julie put her arm around Rob's waist. "I've never seen Leah look this happy. I can't believe how these two met and hit it off right from the start."

Rob smiled and said, "No two people deserve to be happy more than they do."

After dinner, the music for the first dance played, "Septembro," a Brazilian wedding song by Quincy Jones. There were no words to the song. No words were needed. Bill and Leah stood in front of their guests. "May I have this dance?" Bill asked Leah and smiled. She smiled and nodded. He took her hands, then held her in his arms. Leah snuggled into him. She felt herself being consumed in all of Bill's being, and she felt his heart holding her close. This man she loved and who loved her, how beautiful, how perfect, how special and happy he made her. Wrapped in his arms, she knew she was loved and safe forever. Safe and loved as she never thought possible. Bill looked at her, with his beautiful blue eyes. Oh, those eyes that she couldn't resist. She looked at him. She loved him totally. He kissed her lips. He loved her with all his heart, and she knew it. And for the next few minutes, they danced slowly together to the music, safely in each other's presence and seemingly unaware of anything or anyone else around them.

Leah and Bill walked over to Julie and Rob, who were dancing close to them, when the music stopped. "Thank you so much for this," Leah said. "We love you both so much." Bill nodded in agreement. "You've been my rock, Julie. Thank you for your friendship and love. You are my family. You carried me through, and now I've made it. I found happiness. I don't know what I'd have done without you. Julie, Rob, I don't know what else to say. Tonight was the most beautiful night."

"She's right," Bill said. "I couldn't have made it without the two of you either. You brought us together purely by accident. It all played out, all of us unaware of it until it happened. You have been my family and lifeline. Leah and I are at peace now. We made it through some very dark times and then, because of you, found each other."

Julie and Rob just smiled. Rob said, "We love you two so much. This has made us so happy, to see you so happy. We would do anything for you, and you know that. You are our family." They hugged each other, laughing and crying from the love they have kept alive among them. Leah and Bill kissed Rob and Julie. Rob and Julie knew Leah and Bill had finally found the happiness they both so desperately needed. Leah and Bill held Julie's and Rob's hands for a second and then began to mingle through the crowd. Music played, and their guests danced.

Julie and Rob had gone into the house to bring out more food. Julie was almost crying. "Rob, those two are so special. I'm so glad they came to our party that night. It seems like it was just yesterday. She loves him, he loves her, neither one of them really gets what the other has been through, yet they do. Bill loves Leah so much. He adores her. I think she finally gets that he loves her, and nothing else matters. Let's give them one last goodbye before they leave for their honeymoon. Leah confessed that they slept together last night. I don't understand exactly what changed for her, but she said it was beautiful." Julie sighed. "Leah looks different today. Relaxed, and I guess for lack of a better expression, comfortable in her life, like she belongs to this life. That uneasy look in her eyes is gone. She loves that man more than anything. He loves her at least that much. I bought two purple roses for them and forgot I had them. I'm going to find them and have them take them on their honeymoon."

They walked outside, looking for Bill and Leah. Julie took Rob's hand. "I don't see them anywhere. Maybe they went to watch lightning bugs," Rob said and laughed.

Julie noticed a table set up in the corner of the yard. The exact same table in the exact same place where Leah and Bill met. "Did you do this?" she asked Rob as they walked over to the table.

"No, I thought you did," Rob said.

"Wasn't me," Julie said. She shrugged her shoulders. "Oh well, I'll just leave them here. How strange. How romantic." Julie and Rob walked away and tended to their guests.

Bill and Leah were walking through the yard, somehow missing Rob and Julie. They walked to the table that was set up in the far corner of the yard. The table was draped in a satiny off-white table-cloth. Flower petals were scattered on it, along with confetti of stars and hearts. The centerpiece was a small dish with a candle. There was the heart-shaped stain, and of course the two purple roses. Leah touched the table, and she looked at Bill. They smiled at each other. Bill turned to Leah, and he put his arms around her waist. She put her arms around his neck, and they gazed into each other's eyes. Leah put her head on Bill's chest, and as he held her close, they faded from the crowd and into the peace of the night together.

Later that night, after everyone had gone, Julie and Rob were sitting close together on the couch. Rob had his arm around Julie, and her head was resting on his shoulder. They were watching the news on television. "What a beautiful wedding," Julie said to Rob. "They are so happy, finally so happy."

Rob agreed. "I was so worried about Bill for so long. I know you were always worried about Leah. They're perfect for each other." He let out a sigh of relief.

Just then, on the television, came an update on the freeway accident. The newscaster came on and said, "The two victims who were pronounced dead in yesterday's five o'clock tragic freeway accident have been identified as Leah Turner and Bill Stone."

The End

# A Note from the Author

I hope you enjoyed this book.

It seems to have been the trend of thought for some, but not believed by all, that a man who is overweight can't play the romantic lead part and/or the hero in a love story. It wouldn't be believable. Well, not true. It's as true as each day begins. True love is true love. Love has no physical definition. Love defines itself when it's found among two people who are meant to be together.

Please don't judge the people in this story. Each has his or her own personal hell that they deal with, and how they do that is their own way of surviving. It could be drinking, drugs, a weight problem, all of the above. Whatever the case they are desperate to stop the crippling pain even if for just a while, for a few minutes, or even forever.

This story is fiction; the pain I am writing about is not. All they want is to be "normal," a word I hate. What *is* normal? Who decides? The people in this book use their remedies to help kill the pain that is relentless and never quitting to invade their lives. Some handle it differently than others. I guess it depends on the person and their own private hell. Either way, it exhausts them. Their outside is different, be it how they behave or how they look. You get labeled as many things. No one understands why you behave the way you do. Leah and Bill were struggling to stop their hurt.

Their friends are just that, true friends without being asked to be. They accept Bill and Leah as they accept Julie and Rob. They each understand. Julie and Rob had their own walk through hell.

Depression, deep desperation, loneliness, uncontrollable circumstances that throw a person into these coping behaviors have no prejudice. It comes after you with a vengeance, like the devil, a monster, and smothers your every ounce of being. Once it gets hold of you, getting out isn't easy if not impossible. It takes all your strength to cope.

Every heart breaks the same way, and a broken heart can destroy you. A person's heart is their life, and once broken, it's very hard to heal.

Depression takes over you, no matter who you are. It's the same. For some, it's unbearable. They choose remedies to cope and to survive. Others choose to not survive. They have to let go. If they choose to stay, they will be forced to deal with devastating emotional pain, knowing they are not equipped to do so.

Any one of us can be one of the "beautiful ones" and lose it in a New York minute and become one of those who are judged. It could be anyone, anytime.

Every heart is fragile. Every heart, every person, needs someone to love them.

Phyllis was born in 1957 and grew up in Long Island, New York.

Forty-six years ago, she met her husband, who was a professional musician, early one morning at a diner on Long Island, close to the night club where he played in every Sunday night. She and her husband have been married for forty-five years. They have one daughter and one grandson. They moved to Delaware in 1982 and have lived there ever since.

They love animals and have always had a house full of rescue dogs, cats, and even a guinea pig and a tree frog. Horses came into their lives when, at thirty-two, Phyllis decided to learn to ride. This has been something she'd always wanted to do. Shortly after she learned to ride, Phyllis bought her first horse. Then as time went on, she and her husband learned about and became involved in horse rescue. All of their horses after that point were rescues.

Phyllis's favorite sports are softball, baseball, bowling, ice skating and roller skating. She also enjoys watching old movies, especially those in black and white, listening to old radio shows, cooking, gardening, antique cars from the 1920s, 1930s, and 1940s, and music, especially the big bands of the 1940s.

CPSIA information can be obtained
at www.ICGtesting.com
Printed in the USA
LVHW032113260121
677513LV00002B/159